Microsoft Power BI
Query Editor And DAX Programming

In this workbook/guide, we will cover the many behind-the-scenes capabilities of **Power BI.** We will be using the **Power BI Desktop** tool to **Get Data**, the **Power Query Editor** to filter a data source, and the **DAX programming language** to adjust results.

The first step is to use the **Get Data** command in order to extract records from many different data sources such as **Excel, Access, SQL**, etc. Once you **Get Data**, you will then choose a specifically desired table or sheet. Then, you can **Load** all data or **Transform** data to clean up any undesired records.

Databases are becoming very large and now contain more records than what is necessary to build **Reports**. When you choose to **Transform**, it will open the **Query Editor** interface which is used to filter records, correct many database glitches, clean up data, fix anomalies, and transform, or shape data source information. It can also be used to fix misspellings, clarify labels or columns containing wrong data types, automatically merge two data sources into a single table, adjust columns(fields), adjust rows (records), split columns, combine columns, replace information, transpose an entire table, and sort columns.

In these chapters, you will learn the **DAX (Dynamic Analysis Expressions)** program language for business intelligence data modeling and analysis techniques. It will explain how to change the behavior of records and **Reports** based on the **DAX** function and allow you to create new columns that are not already contained in a database. **DAX** contains most of the **Excel** functions, but it also has a built-in record-filtering capability to pull data based on specific criteria. Also, if a user applies a filter in **Power BI**, it might skew the results. However, **DAX** will allow you to extract records and ignore any locally applied filter. The workbook explains **DAX** formula terms, basic structure, and common development techniques. Also included is how to create **New Columns** in a table, custom calculations known as **Measures**, as well as how to create **New Tables.**

Exercise Download

Exercises are posted on the website and can be downloaded to your computer.
Please do the following:

Open Internet Explorer/Edge: Or   Google Chrome:

Type the web address: **elearnlogic.com/download/powerbi-2.exe**

You might get several security warnings, but answer yes and run through each one. When you click "**Unzip**," the files will be located in **C:\Data\PowerBI-2** folder.

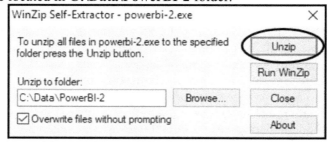

If there are any questions or problems, please contact **Jeff Hutchinson** at: JeffHutch@elearnlogic.com
The following is an alternate download and for Mac users: **elearnlogic.com/download/powerbi-2.zip**

About the Author

Jeff Hutchinson is a computer instructor teaching a variety of classes around the country. He has a BS degree from BYU in Computer-Aided Engineering and has worked in the Information Technology field supporting and maintaining computers for many years. He also previously owned a computer training and consulting firm in San Francisco, California. After selling his business in 2001, he has continued to work as an independent computer instructor around the country. Jeff Hutchinson lives in Utah and also provides training for Utah Valley University Community Education system, offering valuable computer skills for the general knowledge of students, career development, and career advancement. Understanding the technology and the needs of students has been the basis for developing this material. **Jeff Hutchinson** can be contacted at JeffHutch@elearnlogic.com or **(801) 376-6687**.

Table of Contents

Manual Organization

This document is designed for quick navigating of important concepts.
The following are special formatting conventions:

- <u>Table of Contents</u> - This lists every concept covered.
- <u>Numbered Sections</u> - These are located on the left side of a page such as 1.1, 1.2, 1.3, etc.
- <u>Practice Exercises</u> - These contain a **Step-by-Step** approach to demonstrating concepts.
- <u>Student Projects</u> - These projects involve a comprehensive approach to demonstrating concepts.
- <u>Italic Text</u> - This is used to highlight commands that will perform a procedure in the practice exercises.
- <u>Bolded Items</u> - These are important **Concepts,** terminology, and commands used within Excel.
- <u>Tip</u> - These are additional ideas about a concept.
- <u>Index</u> - This is located at the end of the workbook and is used to help reference **Concepts**.

Study Guide For Power BI

The following is a study plan to follow in order to learn necessary core skills of **Power BI**. After these skills are mastered, you can explore your learning as desired.

<u>Chapter 1 - Get Data</u> - One important specific feature is the <u>New Group (1.24)</u> feature which allows you to organize or **Group** items into a single category. Also, in **Section 2** it reviews the <u>Field List More Options</u> in greater detail.

<u>Chapter 2 - Query Editor</u> - This will allow you to manipulate a data source in order to **Transform** or **Shape** data to a specific layout. In other words, this will allow you to change a data type, rename it, and remove columns from being imported into **Power BI**. <u>Section 1</u> is an overview and <u>Section 2</u> demonstrate how to manipulate **Columns**.

<u>Chapter 3 - DAX Formula Overview</u> - This chapter will provide an overview of the most important **DAX** formulas, functions, and capabilities.

<u>Chapter 4 - DAX Reference Guide</u> - Here we will document many common functions and provide practice exercises to demonstrate **DAX** capabilities.

Advanced Topics

<u>Chapter 1 - Get Data</u> - Many students have questions on how to use the
   <u>New Parameter feature (1.64)</u>
<u>Chapter 2 - Query Editor</u> - <u>Section 3</u>, <u>4</u> and <u>5</u> have some interesting capabilities.
<u>Chapter 4 - DAX Reference Guide</u> - The following provide a summary of each section:
   <u>Student Project A - Math And Statistical Summary</u>
   <u>Student Project B - Formatting Functions Summary</u>
   <u>Student Project C - Specialized DAX Functions Summary</u>

Obtain Your PDF Copy and Video Clips

To obtain a **PDF** copy of the courseware and a link to **Online Recorded Video Clips**, send an email to <u>jeffhutch@elearnlogic.com</u> along with a receipt/confirmation email from Amazon. To see an example clip and a list of **Remote Online Courses** available worldwide, go to: <u>www.elearnlogic.com</u>.

Chapter 1 - Get Data

In this chapter, we will cover the first step in the process of getting data to build **Visual Reports**. Here, information can be extracted from a data source to be used in **Power BI Desktop**. Data will be stored in a **Power BI** table, but the table will be connected to a data source that can be refreshed when newly updated data is needed. The screen below is the **Power BI** interface (used to create **Visual Reports)** that is connected to data source. You can then create reports by clicking on the **Report** icon or dragging the field to a work area. The following is a detailed chart describing the process from beginning to end.

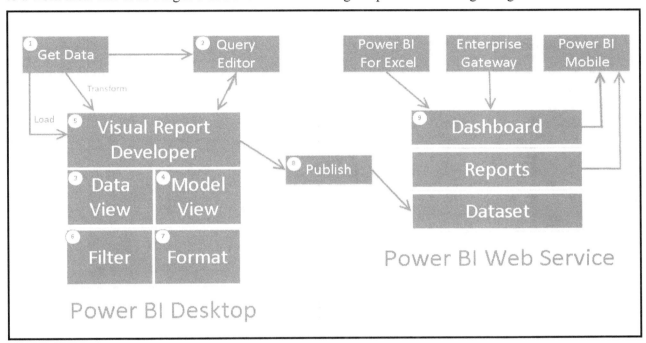

Chapter Table of Contents

Section 1 - Power BI Interface

The following is the Power BI Desktop interface.

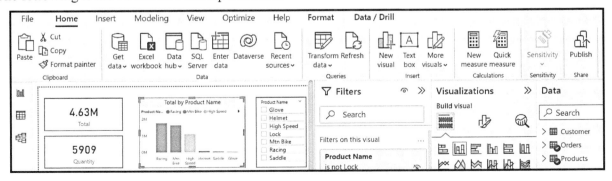

Section Table Of Contents

Practice Exercise 1 - Open BikeDB-B

1. In **Power BI Desktop**: *File Tab →Open Report →* Browse reports →

   C:\Data\PowerBI-2\BikeDB-B.pbix → Open *button*.

   Tip: If you don't have this file, use **BikeDB-B.xlsx** and Load **Load** the data in order to recreate the following **Visual Reports**.

   This will open a Power BI file containing the following Visual Reports:
   Each Power BI file will open a new Power BI program into memory.

2. ***To close the above file, you must exit out of Power BI completely. Also, you must reopen Power BI again in order to work on a different file. To do this, press the ✖ in the upper right corner of the interface.***

1.1 Get Data

This is the first step in the **Get Data** process that supports many data sources including **Excel Spreadsheets**.

1. **Start a new blank Report:** *Start Power BI Desktop or a new blank report (File Tab →* New *).*

2. In **Power BI Desktop:** *Home Ribbon Tab →Data Group →* Get Data.

1.2 Data Source

You can connect to a variety of data sources such as local small databases, larger server-based databases, or data warehouses. A data warehouse is a special type of database that is a storage collection of information and is usually not actively updated. Data can also be extracted from websites such as government census, **Facebook** data, etc. Some of the more common **Data Sources** include **Excel, SQL, Access**, etc. **Power BI** supports many database types. The More... option will display additional connections to data sources.

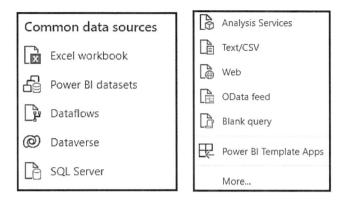

1.3 Load

Load This will skip to the **Query Editor** and Load **Load** directly to the **Visual Report Editor** in the **Power BI Desktop** interface.

1.4 Transform Data

Transform Data This will open the **Query Editor** to adjust a data source by filtering data.

Tip: In previous versions, this button was called Edit .

Practice Exercise 2 - Get Data BikeDB-B

1. **Start a new blank** Report: *Start Power BI Desktop or a new blank report (File Tab → New New).*

2. **Get Data Source:** *Home Ribbon Tab → Data Group → Get Data dropdown arrow → Excel Workbook → C:\Data\PowerBI-2\BikeDB-B.xlsx → Open button.*

3. **Select Sheets:** *Select all 3 sheets from Excel.*

→ Load *button*.

This will skip the **Query Editor** step (filtering data source records) and **Load** data directly to the **Power BI Visual Development Work Area**.

Tip: You can now begin creating **Visual Reports** by clicking a Visual icon and checking Checkboxes in front of the **Field Names**.

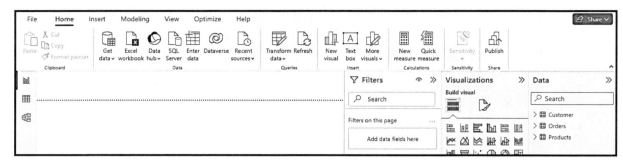

Practice Exercise 3 - Get Data Access Database

This is an optional exercise that requires **Microsoft Access** and **Power BI** to have the same installation option of **32-bit** or **64-bit** (see error below).

1. **Start a new blank Report:** *Start Power BI Desktop or a new blank report (File Tab → New).*

2. **Get Data Source:** *Home Ribbon Tab→ Data Group → Get Data dropdown arrow →*

   More…→Databases → Access Database → Connect →

   C:\Data\PowerBI-2\BikeDB-B.accdb → Open button.

   Tip: Access 32/64 Bit Error - You may receive the following error message when connecting to an **Access** database:

   > Unable to connect
   >
   > We encountered an error while trying to connect.
   >
   > Details: "Microsoft Access: The 'Microsoft.ACE.OLEDB.12.0' provider is not registered on the local machine. The 64-bit version of the Access Database Engine 2010 Access Database Engine OLEDB provider may be required to read 'Northwind 2016.accdb'. To download the client software, visit the following site: https://go.microsoft.com/fwlink/?LinkID=285987."

   This indicates that the installed version of **Access** is **32-bit** and **Power BI** has been installed using a **64-bit** (or the opposite case will also produce the error). This mismatched error can be resolved by installing **Power BI** or **Access** using the same installation style (32-bit or 64-bit). If you are still receiving an error using the **32-bit** installation of **Access** and **Power BI**, then install the following from the **Microsoft** website: **Microsoft Access Database Engine 2010 Redistributable**. If you receive an error, use the following file:

   C:\Data\PowerBI-2\BikeDB-B.xlsx.

3. **Select Access Tables:** *Select all 3 Tables from the Access Database.*

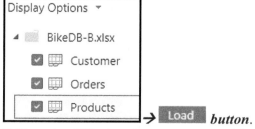

   → Load button.

   This will skip the **Query Editor** step (filtering data source records) and **Load** data directly to the **Power BI Visual Development Work Area.**

1.5 Undo/Redo Ribbon Group

This is the menu command located on the top of the interface.

Undo is located in the upper left corner of the interface in the **Quick Access Toolbar**. As you create new **Visual Reports,** the following will **Undo** and **Redo** steps performed:

Undo - This fixes mistakes. Shortcut: $\boxed{\text{Ctrl}}$ $\boxed{\text{Z}}$ keys.

Redo - This reverses the **Undo**. Shortcut: $\boxed{\text{Ctrl}}$ $\boxed{\text{Y}}$ keys.

Tip: Each consecutive $\boxed{\text{Ctrl}}$ $\boxed{\text{Z}}$ keys will **Undo** multiple steps and choose $\boxed{\text{Ctrl}}$ $\boxed{\text{Y}}$ key **Redo.**

1.6 Blank Query SQL Code

This will allow you to **Cut** n **Paste** a **SQL** code into the **Blank Query** option. The code will contain a connection to the database.

Section 2 - Field List More Options

A **Field List** is located on the right side of an interface. This entire section describes things that can be accomplished a the **Field List**. For example, you **Right-click** on any field or press ⋯ **More Options**, a **Context** menu will appear with many choices. This **Section** will review these ⋯ **More Options** in greater detail.

Tip: The **Dec 2018 Update** added the Alt Shift F10 keys to expand ⋯ **More Options** in a Field List. Also, you can use the Arrow key to navigate and open fields in a table. The Space Bar key will then select a highlighted field to be used in a report.

Section Table Of Contents

Practice Exercise 4 - Load BikeDB-B

1. **Begin a new blank** ⬚ **Report:** Start **Power BI Desktop** or a new blank report (*File Tab →* New *New*).

2. ⬚ **Get Data Source:** *Home Ribbon Tab →Data Group →* ⬚ *Get Data dropdown arrow →*

Excel Workbook → C:\Data\PowerBI-2\BikeDB-B.xlsx → Open *. Select all 3 Sheets →*

 → Load *button*.

1.7 Field Type

The **Field List** is located on the right side of an interface. It contains a list of field columns in a data set. The following are the definition of **Icons** displayed next to the **Field** showing a **Field Type.** The most commonly used are ∑ Numeric Data Type, ▦ Data Data Type, and ▦ New Column:

📈 **KPI**   🅰️= **Identity Fields**   ▦ **New Measure**   ▦ **Numeric Calculated Columns**

🌐 **Map field**   🖩 **Measure Groups**   ▦ **New Column**   ▦? **Parameter Fields**

▦ **Groups**   ▦ **Date Data Type**   🔖 **Hierarchy**   ∑ **Numeric Data Type**

📁 **Folders**   ▦ **Calculated Tables**   ⚠ **Warning**   ▦ **Non-Numeric Calculated Columns**

Tip: These icons were added in the **Nov 2020 Update**.
Tip: The **Feb 2021 Update** increased the size of **Icons** in front of **Fields** defining **Data Types**.

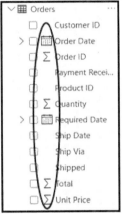

1.8 Field Checkbox

This will select the ☑ checkbox in front of the highlighted field.

1.9 Create Hierarchy

This will create a **New Field** in the **Field List** that has a common **Hierarchical** logical relationship. Each **Hierarchical** field will provide an additional related level of detail. **Tip:** Refer to the **Hierarchical Drill-Down** capability located in:
Power BI Desktop Workbook - Chapter 4 Section 3 (Create Hierarchy).

Practice Exercise 5 - Complicated Matrix

1. **Begin a new blank** ▦ **Report:** Start **Power BI Desktop** or a new blank report (*File Tab* → New *New*).

2. ▦ **Get Data Source:** *Home Ribbon Tab* →*Data Group* → ▦ *Get Data dropdown arrow* →

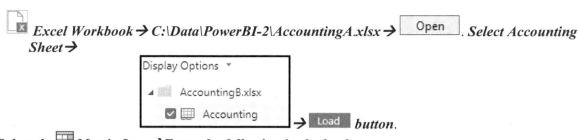

Excel Workbook → C:\Data\PowerBI-2\AccountingA.xlsx → Open . *Select Accounting Sheet →*

→ Load *button.*

3. *Select the ▦ Matrix Icon → Enter the following in the buckets.*

Rows

| Country | ∨ × |
| Customer Type | ∨ × |

Columns

| Month | ∨ × |

Values

| Sum of GrossSales | ∨ × |

4. *The results will look like the following:*

Country	1	2	3	4	5	6	7	8	9	10	11	12	Total
⊞ Canada	90,654.33	11,860.50				8,363.04	11,882.22	19,758.48		602.49		24,163.44	167,284.50
⊞ China	3,020.43	7,909.50								3,000.48	12,384.96		26,315.37
⊞ England	1,775.55	4,644.00		11,590.95				23,943.99		5,454.33			47,408.82
⊟ France		71,007.70	56,207.36					9,971.01				138,462.83	275,648.90
Large		20,359.20	3,977.03									27,909.07	52,245.30
Medium		11,906.14	4,451.08					9,971.01				22,165.58	48,493.81
Midmarket		12,759.43	14,915.11									27,625.26	55,299.80
Small		21,931.05	22,325.26									24,555.48	68,811.79
Small Business		4,051.88	10,538.88									36,207.44	50,798.20
⊞ Germany	2,433.90	4,560.00	13,509.87					21,518.07			5,808.00		47,829.84
⊞ Mexico	58,248.49	10,519.50						8,414.91		570.57	3,383.52		81,136.99
⊞ USA	104,819.94					67,698.33	77,968.59	87,835.86	94,694.67	81,980.71		201,038.47	716,036.57
Total	260,952.64	110,501.20	69,717.23	11,590.95	67,698.33	86,331.63	99,718.08	178,301.13	81,980.71	9,627.87	21,576.48	363,664.74	1,361,660.99

1.10 New Measure

▦ Measures are a **DAX** formula created to analyze data using functions such as **Sums**, **Averages**, **Minimum** or **Maximum** values, **Counts**, static values, or more advanced calculations. **Tip:** Refer to the **New Measures** capability located in: **Power BI Pro Web Workbook** or **Power BI Desktop Workbook Chapter 6 Section 1 (New Measure)**.

1.11 New Column

This will create a ▦ **New Column (Field)** to an existing table that contains a mathematical formula providing valuable information. The programming language used is called **Data Analysis Expression (DAX)**. **Tip:** Refer to the **New Column** capability located in: **Power BI Desktop Workbook Chapter 6 Section 1 (New Column)**.

1.12 New Quick Measure

▦ You can use ▦ **Quick Measures** to quickly and easily create common, powerful calculations. **Quick Measure** opens a dialog box, you choose the options, then it creates a **New Measure** to be used in your report.

1.13 Rename

This **Renames** a **Field Name** located in a **Field List**. *Select the* [···] *More Options (or Right-Click) on the desired field →Rename.*

1.14 Delete From Model

This **Deletes** the **Field** or **Table** located in a **Field List**. To reverse this deletion, go to the **Query Editor** and remove the **Applied Step** which is called **Remove Columns** ☒ Removed Columns. *Select the* [···] *More Options (or Right-Click) on the desired field →Delete from Model.*
Tip: The **Oct 2021 Update** added an ability to remove a table from a **Field List**.
   Right-click on the table in the field list →Delete From Model.

1.15 Hide Field Name

This feature will allow you to **Hide Field Names** that are unusable and taking up space in the **Field List**. When you **Hide** them, the **Field List** will be shorter. However, if a **Field** is used in a **Visual Report** and then is **Hidden**, it will still be actively displayed in the **Visual Report**.
Select the [···] *More Options (or Right-Click) on the desired field →Choose Hide.*

Practice Exercise 6 - Hide Field

In the Field List: *Select the* [···] *More Options (or Right-Click) on the* ☑ Country
   field →Choose the Hide option. **Tip:** The **Field** will disappear from the **Field List**.

1.16 View Hidden

This will allow you to display s **Hidden** field. Although the field will appear with an 🖾 icon next to the field name, you will only see a dimmed version of the field. Example: ☐ Σ Year 🖾.
However, after a field is **Hidden**, it can become **Visible** which takes two steps:
1. **View Hidden fields:** *Turn on the View Hidden* ☑ View hidden *Check.*
2. **Unhide the specific desired field:** *Once the* ☑ View hidden *is checked, then uncheck the* ☑ Hide *To* ☐ Hide
Tip: Hidden fields that are **Visible** can be used to create **Visual Reports** (not hidden fields).

Practice Exercise 7 - Unhide Field

There are several steps to **Hide** and **Unhide** a field:
1. **Hide the Region field:** *Select the* [···] *More Options (or Right-Click) on the* ☑ Region
   field → Choose the ☑ Hide *option.* **Tip:** The **Field** should disappear.

2. **View Hidden Fields:** *Right-Click any field* → *Check or turn on the* ✓ View hidden .
   Tip: The ☑ Region field should be **Visible**. ☑ Region
3. **Unhide Fields:** *Right-Click on the* ☑ Region *Hidden field* → *Turn off the Hide Checkbox* Hide .

1.17 Unhide All

If any field is **Hidden,** this feature will **Unhide** all fields.

1.18 Collapse All

This **Collapses Field List Fieldnames** under a **Database Name**. When you select ⋯ **More Options** (or **Right-Click** on a field) in a **Field List,** an option is available to **Collapse/Expand** all fields. **Tip:** The **Dec 2018 Update** added the Alt Left-Arrow keyboard command to **Collapse** a selected table in a **Field List**. Also, the Alt Shift 1 keys will **Collapse** a **Field List**.

∨ ⊞ Customer
∨ ⊞ Orders
∨ ⊞ Products

1.19 Expand All

This **Expands Field List Fieldnames** under a **Database Name**. When you select ⋯ **More Options** (or **Right-Click** on a field) in the **Field List,** an option is available to **Collapse/Expand** all fields. **Tip:** The **Dec 2018 Update** added the Alt Right-Arrow keyboard command to **Expand** a table in a **Field List**. Also, the Alt Shift 9 keys will **Expand** a **Field List**.

∧ ⊞ Customer
☐ Address1
☐ Address2
☐ City

1.20 New Group

In **Power BI**, you can **Group** Records in a **Text** field to more clearly view, analyze, explore data and trends in your **Visuals**. For example, you might want to categorize a list of **Products** into several **Groups** such as **Products** and **Accessories**. The **Group** feature will create a **New Field** in the **Field List**. For example, you can **Group** several records inside a **Field**. For instance, the **Northern America Group** could contain USA, Mexico, and Canada and **European Group** could contain France, Germany, and England.

1. *Right-click on the field to be Grouped in a Field List, then Right-click to choose a New Group option.*
2. **Create New Group** - This will allow you to create a **New Group** from **Ungrouped** values (left side of the dialog box). *Select Ungrouped values by using the* Ctrl *key to choose several items, then press the* Group *button.*

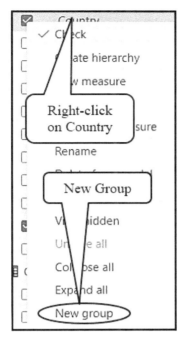

Practice Exercise 8 - Group Chart

Continue using the **BikeDB-B** data source.

Here, we will create two groups: **Northern America** and all other countries.

1. **Create a New Group:** *Right-Click on the* Country *field→New Group.*

The following dialog box will appear:

2. **Select the Countries:** *Hold the* Ctrl *key down and select the desired countries→Select Canada, Mexico, and USA→Press the* Group *button.*

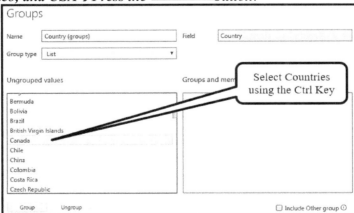

3. **Rename a Group:** *Double-Click on the Group Name and rename it to Northern America →Check:*  *→* **OK** .

4. **Create A Pie Chart:**

4a. *Click on the white area to make sure nothing is selected.*

4b. **Create a Pie Chart:** *Click on the* ⬤ *Pie Chart icon.*

4c. **Drag Fields:** *Drag a* ☑ ⊞ Country (groups) *field to the Details Bucket and the Orders/* ☑ ∑ Total *field to the Values Bucket.*

1.21 Edit Groups

⊞ Once a **Group** has been created, it can be **Edited** by: *Right-Clicking on the Group Field* ☑ ⊞ Country (groups) *(located in the Field List), then choose Edit Group.* The following dialog box will appear to make changes to the **Group:**

The following **Group Edit** options are available:

1. **Rename Group** - *Double-Click on the Group title in the Name box.*
2. **Remove A Group** - *Select a Group from Groups and Members and press the*

`Ungroup` *Ungroup button.*

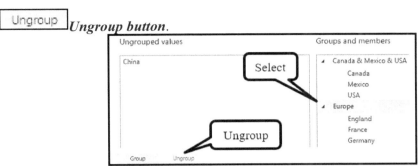

Tip: In order to add a **Country** to an existing **Group** you must **Ungroup**, select the countries, then create a new **Group**.

3. **Add to Group** - This will allow you to add an **Ungrouped** item to an existing **Group**. *Select the Ungrouped value → Select the existing Group (Groups and Members) → Click the* `Group` *Group button.*

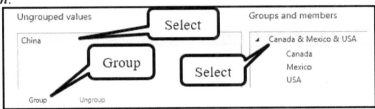

4. **Remove Field** - To **Remove** a **Field** from a **Group**: Select it from the **Groups and Members** box and then click **Ungroup**. You can also select whether **Ungrouped** categories should be placed into **Other Groups**, or if they should remain **Ungrouped**.

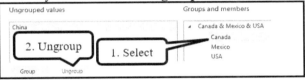

Practice Exercise 9 - Get Data BikeDB-B Pie Chart

1. **Begin a new blank** 🗒 **Report:** Start **Power BI Desktop** or a new blank report (*File Tab →* `New` *New*).

2. 🗒 **Get Data Source:** *Home Ribbon Tab →Data Group →* 🗒*Get Data dropdown arrow →* 📄 *Excel Workbook → C:\Data\PowerBI-2\BikeDB-B.xlsx →* `Open` *→Select all 3 Sheets →*

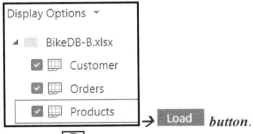

→ `Load` *button.*

3. **Create A Pie Chart:** *Click on the* 🥧 *Pie Chart.*

4. **Drag Fields:** *Drag fields to the following Bucket positions: Customer/* ✓ `Country` *and Orders/* ✓ ∑ `Total`

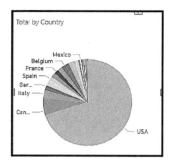

Practice Exercise 10 - Select Group

Continue using the **BikeDB-B** data source.
1. *Click in the white area to unselect all Visual Reports*.

2. **Create a Pie Chart:** *Create a Pie Chart by clicking on the* Pie Chart icon.

3. **Drag Fields:** *Drag the fields Customer/* Country *and Orders/* ∑ Total *to the Bucket positions (below)*.

4. **Create a Group:** *Hold the* Ctrl *key down and select several bars* → *Select USA, Mexico, and Canada*.

5. **Group the selected items:** *Right-Click on USA* → *Choose Group or Data/Drill Ribbon Group* →

Group button. The chart will then be divided into 2 groups.

Before (Step 1,2,3)	After (Step 4,5)

1.22 Edit Clusters

The **Cluster** feature will identify closely related data in a **Table** or **Matrix** and group or **Cluster** them together. The **Edit Clusters** feature will allow you to change the name and the **Clusters**. **Tip:** Refer to the **Edit Clusters** capability located in:

Power BI Desktop Workbook - Chapter 4 Section 2 (Edit Clusters).

1.23 Add To Filters

This is a way to add a **Filter** to a **Visual-Level**, **Page-Level**, or **Report-Level Filter**. In order to use the **Visual-Level Filters,** you must select the desired **Visual Report**.
Right-click on any field in the field list or ***Choose the*** ⬚⬚⬚ .

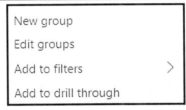

More Options. **Tip:** Refer to the **Filter Report** capability located in:
   Power BI Desktop Workbook - Chapter 4 Section 1 (Add Filter).

1.24 Add To Drill Through

Add the selected field to the **Drill Through Bucket**.
Tip: Refer to the **Drill Through** capability located in:
Power BI Desktop Workbook - Chapter 4 Section 3 (Drill Through).

New group	
Edit groups	
Add to filters	>
Add to drill through	

1.25 Copy Table

This will make a copy of a table to be used independently from the origional.

Practice Exercise 11 – Copy Table

In Power BI: *Open the* ▦ *Data View (located in the upper left side of interface)* →

Right-click on table name (located on the right side of the interface in the field list) → Copy table .

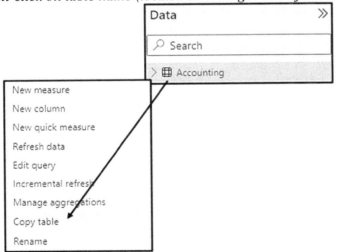

Section 3 - Report View / Home Ribbon Tab

The 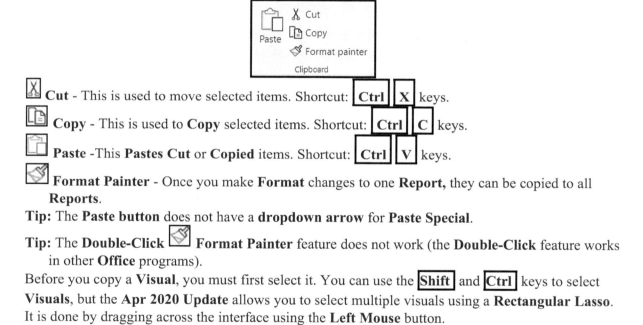 **Report View / Home Ribbon Tab** is located on the left side of the interface. A **Nov 2019 Update** changed the interface to operate similar to the **Office Suite** functionality. Before **Nov 2019,** when buttons on the ribbon were disabled, they were grayed out. Now, they disappear when you switch between ribbons (this is called a **Contextual Ribbon Tab**). The ribbon will now collapse or expand to a single line (see ⌃ in the upper right corner of the ribbon). Also, more contextual ribbons will appear providing options for a specific purpose such as **Format** and **Data/Drill Ribbon Tab**.

Section Table Of Contents

1.26 Clipboard Ribbon Group

Cut - This is used to move selected items. Shortcut: **Ctrl** **X** keys.

Copy - This is used to **Copy** selected items. Shortcut: **Ctrl** **C** keys.

Paste -This **Pastes Cut** or **Copied** items. Shortcut: **Ctrl** **V** keys.

Format Painter - Once you make **Format** changes to one **Report,** they can be copied to all **Reports**.

Tip: The **Paste button** does not have a **dropdown arrow** for **Paste Special**.

Tip: The **Double-Click** **Format Painter** feature does not work (the **Double-Click** feature works in other **Office** programs).

Before you copy a **Visual**, you must first select it. You can use the **Shift** and **Ctrl** keys to select **Visuals**, but the **Apr 2020 Update** allows you to select multiple visuals using a **Rectangular Lasso**. It is done by dragging across the interface using the **Left Mouse** button.

1.27 Get Data

This is the first step in the process to **Get Data** in order to create a **Dashboard**. The system supports many data sources including an **Excel Spreadsheet**.

Practice Exercise 12 - Get Data AccountingB

1. **Begin a new blank Report:** *Start Power BI Desktop or a new blank report (File Tab→* New *New).*

2. **Get Data Source:** *Home Ribbon Tab→Data Group→Get Data dropdown arrow →* Excel Workbook → *C:\Data\PowerBI-2\AccountingB.xlsx →* Open *button.*

3. **Select an Excel Sheet:** *Choose the* ☑ *Accounting Sheet.*

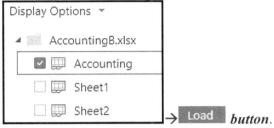

→ Load *button.*

This will skip the **Query Editor** step (filtering data source records) and **Load** data directly to a **Power BI Visual Development Work Area** in order to build **Visual Reports.**

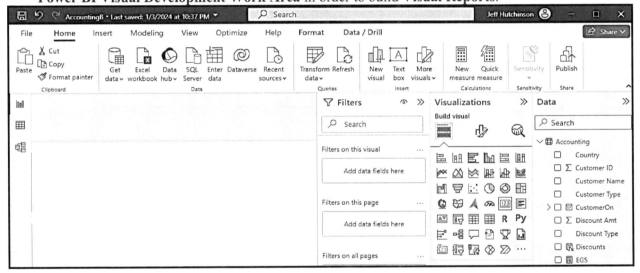

Practice Exercise 13 - From Web

This will extract a database from a **Web** site.

1. **In Power BI Desktop:** *Get Data dropdown →* Web *→*
   URL: **https://www.bankrate.com/retirement/best-and-worst-states-for-retirement/**

→ OK .

2. *Select the folowing table and then choose Transform:*

```
Display Options ▾                                        ⬒
 ◢ 🗀  HTML Tables [1]
   ☑ ⊞  Best and worst states to retire in 2023
```
→ Load .

*3. **Make sure the data is loaded into Power BI(Choose Apply Changes if necessary) →Home Ribbon***

Tab→Queries Group→ [⊞] ***Transform Data.***

*4. **Home Ribbon Tab→ Transform Group→*** Use First Row as Headers ▾ .

*5. **Select "5 Best States To Retire" →Add Column Ribbon Tab →General Group →***
[⊡ Duplicate Column]

*6. **Select "5 Best States To Retire" →Transform Ribbon Tab →Text Column Group→*** ABC 123 Extract ▾ →
[First Characters] ***→1.***

Extract First Characters

Enter how many starting characters to keep.

Count

| 1| |

*7. **Select "5 Best Styates To Retire-Copy" → Transform Ribbon Tab →Text Column Group →***
ABC 123 Extract ▾ → Text After Delimiter ***→Type a space in the box below***

Text After Delimiter

Enter the delimiter that marks the beginning of what you would like to extract.

Delimiter

| |

*8. **Select "5 Worst States To Retire" →Add Column Ribbon Tab →General Group →***
[⊡ Duplicate Column]

*9. **Select "5 Worst States To Retire" →Transform Ribbon Tab →Text Column***
Group→ ABC 123 Extract ▾ → First Characters ***→2.***

Extract First Characters

Enter how many starting characters to keep.

Count

| 2| |

*10. **Select "5 Worst States To Retire-Copy" → Transform Ribbon Tab →Text Column Group →***
ABC 123 Extract ▾ → Text After Delimiter ***→Type a space in the box below***

Text After Delimiter

Enter the delimiter that marks the beginning of what you would like to extract.

Delimiter

| |

11. *Rename lables to Best States, Best Priority, Worst States, Worst Priority*

	A^B_C Best Priority	A^B_C Worst Priority	A^B_C Best States	A^B_C Worst States
1	1	50	Iowa	Alaska
2	2	49	Delaware	New York
3	3	48	West Virginia	California
4	4	47	Missouri	Washington
5	5	46	Mississippi	Massachusetts

12. Home Ribbon Tab→Close Group→ *Close & Apply.*

13. *Create a table and place the fields in a the Values Bucket.*

Best States	Best Priority	Worst States	Worst Priority
Delaware	2	New York	49
Iowa	1	Alaska	50
Mississippi	5	Massachusetts	46
Missouri	4	Washington	47
West Virginia	3	California	48

1.28 Excel Workbook

This will import data from **Excel** using the **Get Data** capability.

1.29 Data Hub

This creates a live connection to datasets that have been published in **Power BI Pro Web Service**.

Practice Exercise 14 - Power BI Data Hub

1. **Start a new blank Report:** *Start Power BI Desktop or a new blank report (File Tab →* New *New).*

2. Report View →Home Ribbon Tab →Data Group → *Power BI Datasets →Select a Dataset (below):*

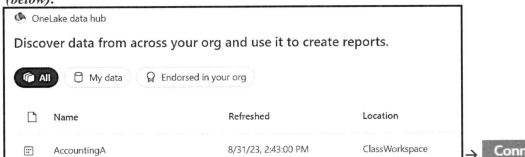

3. Choose the actual record you want to connect to→Select Country.

Tip: This assumes you have previously published a **Power BI Desktop** file to **Power BI Pro Web**.

1.30 SQL Server

It will import data or establish a **DirectQuery** connection to a **SQL data source**.

1.31 Enter Data

This will create a new blank **Table** and allow you to enter new data. **To create the Table:**

1. **In Power BI:** *Home Ribbon Tab →Queries Group →* *Transform Data*.

2. **In the Power Query Editor:** *Home Ribbon Tab →New Query Group →* *Enter Data*.

To Edit the Table: *In Power BI →Home Ribbon Tab → Queries Group →* *Transform Data →*
Select Table →Applied Steps → Source → *Gear →(Edit the fields in the Table) →* OK *button.*

Practice Exercise 15 - Enter Data

Create a **New Table** and **Enter Data**.

In **Power BI**: *Home Ribbon Tab → Data Group →* 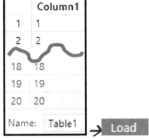 *Enter Data → Enter values 1 through 20 →*
Name: Table1 →

Tip: The **New Table**, called **Table1**, will be in a **Field List** located on the right side of the interface.

1.32 Dataverse

This is a cloud-based database environment and contains **Tables** similar to **Excel**. It is used as the backbone for the **Power App** platform but can also contain data storage for business data. **Dataverse** was previously called **Common Data Service (CDS)**. However, this product will not be covered in the workbook.

1.33 Recent Sources

After you have opened a data source, it will be listed under the **Recent Sources** button. This is a shortcut to a previously accessed data source.

In **Power BI**: *Home Ribbon Tab → Data Group → Recent Sources*.

1.34 Transform Data

This will open the **Query Editor** to filter information coming into **Power BI**. This will allow you to **Transform**, shape, of eliminating unwanted records.

When finished, choose **Close & Apply**.

Practice Exercise 16 - Transform Data

1. In **Power BI**: *Home Ribbon Tab →Queries Group →* Transform Data Dropdown arrow→ *Transform Data.*

2. **In Power Query Editor**: *Home Ribbon Tab →Close Group →* Close & Apply.

1.35 Refresh

The **Refresh** button is located in **Power BI** as well as **Power Query Editor**. If **Power BI Desktop** is connected to a local data source, it will get newly updated data connected to a live database or through a gateway. A **Refresh** will get new data from the data source and **Refresh** all **Visual Reports**.

Tip: The **Power BI Pro Web Service** product has the ability to connect to the **Power BI Gateway** product which will allow automatic updates on a scheduled basis.

1.36 New Visual

This creates a **New Blank Visual Report**. The report below is a report template that contains no data source. As soon as you apply a data source field to the template, it will report on the information.

1.37 TextBox

This can be used to create a title for a **Visual Report** or **Dashboard**. It can also be placed on a **Visual Report** to clarify the information displayed. When you add a **TextBox**, the following **Contextual Text Ribbon Tab** will be displayed:

In Power BI: *Home Ribbon Tab →Insert Group →* Text Box→

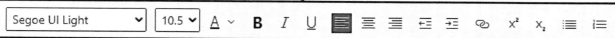

Practice Exercise 17 - Text Box

When you select a **TextBox,** the following toolbar popup will appear:

In Power BI: *Home Ribbon Tab →Insert Group →*  *TextBox →Draw the TextBox in the work area.*

1.38 More Visuals

This will take you to the **App Source Website** in order to add additional **Apps** to **Power BI Desktop**.

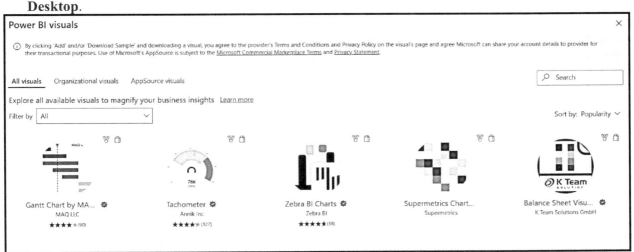

1.39 New Measure

Measures are a **DAX** formula created to analyze data using functions such as **Sums**, **Averages**, **Minimum** or **Maximum** values, **Counts**, static values, and more advanced calculations. Refer to the **New Measures** capability located in:
Power BI Desktop Workbook - Chapter 6 Section 1 (New Measure).

1.40 Quick Measure

You can use Quick Measures to quickly and easily create common, powerful calculations. **Quick Measure** opens a dialog box, you choose the options, then it creates a **New Measure** to be used in your report.

1.41 Sensitivity

This must first be enabled in the **Admin Center**. The feature will ensure that authorized users will be able to see all **Reports**, **Dashboards**, **Datasets**, and **Dataflows**. Setting the **Sensitivity** level will ensure that only authorized users in the organization will be able to see and access your data. However, these **Sensitivity** levels will not be covered in this workbook.

1.42 Publish

This will **Publish** reports to the **Power BI Pro Web Service** available on the internet for others to view.

Section 4 - Report View / Insert Ribbon Tab

The **Insert Ribbon Tab** is used to insert objects such as **New Page, AI Visuals, Text Box, Buttons, Shapes, Images**, etc.

Section Table Of Contents

1.43 New Page

This creates a **New Page** or duplicates an existing page. However, an easier way to create a New page is to **Right-click** on the ![+] **Page** icon located on the bottom of the interface.

1.44 New Visual

This creates a **New Blank Visual Report**. The report below is a report template that contains no data source. As soon as you apply a data source field to the template, it will report on the information.

1.45 More Visuals

This will take you to the **App Source Website** to add additional custom **Visuals** available in **Power BI Desktop**.

1.46 Q&A Button

This will add a **Visual** to allow you to **Ask A Question** about a data source. You can use natural language to **Ask A Question** or just type in keywords. It will generate a report related to all information entered. See **Power BI Pro Web Workbook - Chapter 4 Section 4 (Question and Answer)** for more details.

Practice Exercise 18 - Q&A Button

1. ***Click in the white work area to create a new report.***

2. **Create a Q&A:** *Select the* [□] *Q&A button.*
3. ***Type keywords to display a Report: Type: Canada Customer Name.***
   Tip: A **Blue** underline means it recognized the keyword
   Tip: A **Red** underline means it did not recognize the keyword.

4. **Finalize Report:** *Press* [□] *to finalize the report.*

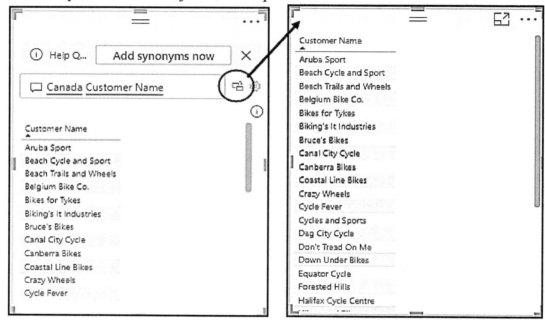

1.47 Key Influencers

This will analyze data based on a **Key** numeric or measure field. When you specify fields you want to analyze, the result will display fields that **Influence** the **Key** numeric field the most.

1.48 Decomposition Tree

This feature was added in **Nov 2019 Update**. It will create a **Tree** layout expanding elements to be **Analyzed**. Refer to the following for more details: **Power BI Desktop Workbook - Chapter 4 Section 3 (Decomposition).**

1.49 Smart Narrative

This creates a summarized statement about your **Visuals**. It provides relevant insights that display trends and keys to other points of interest.

At 716,036.57, USA had the highest GrossSales and was 2,620.98% higher than China, which had the lowest GrossSales at 26,315.37.

Practice Exercise 19 - Smart Narrative Button

1. **Create a Stacked Column Chart:**

   1a. ***Click in the white area and unselect all Visual Reports.***

   1b. ***Click on the*** [Stacked Column Chart icon] ***Stacked Column Chart icon.***

   1c. **Drag Fields:** *Drag Fields to the following Bucket positions:*

2. **Select the Stacked Column Chart:** *Insert Ribbon Tab →AI Visuals Group →* [icon] *Smart Narrative or choose the* [icon] *Smart Narrative icon in the available Visualizations.*

   > At 3,210,946.68, USA had the highest Sum of Total and was 9,730,041.45% higher than Nepal, which had the lowest Sum of Total at 33.
   >
   > Sum of Total and total Sum of Last Year's Sales are positively correlated with each other.
   >
   > USA accounted for 69.34% of Sum of Total.
   >
   > Sum of Total and Sum of Last Year's Sales diverged the most when the Country was USA, when Sum of Total were 850,545.99 higher than Sum of Last Year's Sales.

1.50 Paginated Report (Preview)

[icon] A **Paginated Report** is designed for a printable or **PDF** page layout and can be created using **Power BI Report Builder**. One advantage is that you can create a multiple-page **PDF** file, while the standard **Power BI** will only create one page. Formatting is different because each element in a report is formatted using properties and the file is saved with an extension of .rdl. This allows you to get a data source to develop charts, format, and filters similar to **Power BI Desktop**. You can also publish the **Paginated Report** to **Power BI Pro Web Service** or add it to **Power BI Desktop**.

1.51 Power Apps

[icon] In order to use the **Power BI Power App** icon, a **Power App** must be created outside of **Power BI**. This **Office 365 App** feature is used to create additional functionality in order to perform a specific purpose. Once an **App** is created, it can be added to **Power BI Desktop** using the **Power App** icon. However, the **App** must be developed first before it can be applied to the **Power BI Desktop** icon. An **App** can be connected to a database or **Excel** table of information. It then can be used to modify or add new records to a data source using a form style input screen. Note: The **App** development will not be covered in this workbook.

1.52 Power Automate

This will automate redundant tasks and perform them all with a click of a button. For example, send an email to a selected or filtered record from **Power BI**, post information on YouTube, or copy information and save it to a specific file name. This is available in **Office 365** but is also now available in **Power BI**. It uses many of the modules defined in **Office 365**. However, the **Power Automate** feature is beyond the scope of this workbook.

Tip: **Power Automate** was previously called **Flow** in **Office 365**.

Practice Exercise 20 - Power Automate

1. **Create a Stacked Column Chart:**
   1a. *Click in the white area and unselect all Visual Reports.*

   1b. *Click on the Stacked Column Chart icon.*

   1c. **Drag Fields:** *Drag Fields to the following Bucket positions:*

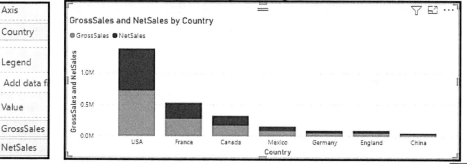

2. *Select the Stacked Column Chart →Insert Ribbon Tab →Power Platform Group → Power Automate.*

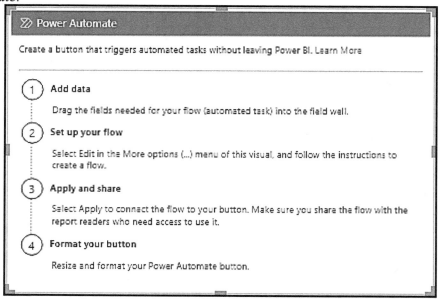

1.53 TextBox

This can be used to create a title for a **Visual Report** or **Dashboard**. **Text Boxes** can be added to **Charts** for clarification of what was charted. When you add or select a **TextBox**, the following **Contextual Text Ribbon Tab** will be displayed: ***Insert Ribbon Tab→Elements Group→ Text Box→***

Practice Exercise 21 - Text Box

When you select **TextBox,** the following toolbar popup will appear:
Insert Ribbon Tab→Elements Group→ TextBox→Draw the TextBox in the work area.

My New Reports

Tip: The icon will allow you to add a hyperlink to the text.

1.54 Buttons

Buttons will help with navigation and provide additional information. You can also add an **Image** and make changes to the **Format Action** option applied to an **Image**.

Tip: You can also search the internet for a back-arrow image, add the arrow image to **Power BI,** then apply the navigation using **Format Image** tools.

Tip: The **Sep 2021 Update** added additional **Buttons**. An **Image** can also be defined as a **Custom Button** (*Format Pane→* ⌄ Action [On] *→* ⌄ Action *→Type*).

In **Format Pane,** you can apply the following option which will allow a **Button** to navigate back to its original location. ***Insert Ribbon Tab→Elements Group→ button→ Back→Select button→ Format Pane (located on the right side of the interface)***.

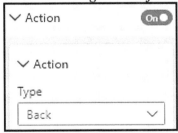

← **Left Arrow** - This will display the **Left Arrow** button and can be reassigned to the following actions: Back, Bookmark, Drill Through, Q&A, and Web URL.

→ **Right Arrow** - This will display the **Right Arrow** button and can be reassigned to the following actions: Back, Bookmark, Drill Through, Q&A, and Web URL.

↰ **Reset -** This will display the **Reset Arrow** button and can be reassigned to the following actions: Back, Bookmark, Drill Through, Q&A, and Web URL.

↩ **Back** - By default, this will navigate back to the previous page. However, you can reassign the button to the following actions: Back, Bookmark, Drill Through, Q&A, and Web URL.

ⓘ **Information** - This will display the **Information** button and can be reassigned to the following actions: Back, Bookmark, Drill Through, Q&A, and Web URL.

⑦ **Help** - This will display the **Help** button and can be reassigned to the following actions: Back, Bookmark, Drill Through, Q&A, and Web URL.

▭ **Q&A Button** - By default, this will display the **Q&A Visual Report**, but it can also be reassigned to the following actions: Back, Bookmark, Drill Through, Q&A, and Web URL.

🔖 *Bookmark* - This will display the **Bookmark** button and can be reassigned to the following actions: Back, Bookmark, Drill Through, Q&A, and Web URL.
Refer to the following for more details: **Power BI Desktop Workbook - Chapter 5 Section 4 (Bookmark Pane).**

▭ *Blank* - This will allow you to define a custom button and reassign the following actions: Back, Bookmark, Drill Through, Q&A, and Web URL.

Practice Exercise 22 - Web Link Button

1. *Insert Ribbon Tab→Elements Group→* ▭ *button→* ▭ *Blank.*
2. *Select button→* ▭ *Format Pane (located on the right side of the interface) →* (▭ *Format Pane→* ▭ Action — On ● → ▭ Action →Enter the following options:*

Tip: Refer to the following for more details: **Power BI Desktop Workbook - Chapter 4 - Section 3 (Drill Through Button).**

1.55 Shapes

▭ **Shapes** can be added to point to or identify specific **Visual Reports**. You can use the **Rectangle Shape** as a frame to relate two or more **Visual Reports**. However, you will need to set the **Format Fill Transparency** to **100%**.

The **Rectangle** tool can be used to identify or encircle several related reports. **Tip:** Format the background to 100% transparency in order to see the **Reports** inside the rectangle.

Tip: The **Apr 2021 Update** added new **Shapes** and increased the formatting options available.

Practice Exercise 23 - Shapes

1. **Identify two Visual Reports.**

2. **Add a Rectangle:** *Insert Ribbon Tab →Elements Group →* 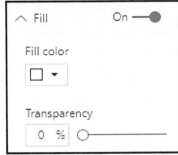 *Shapes*

   Dropdown → ☐ *Rectangle.*
3. **Adjust the Rectangle:** *Positions it around the two Visual Reports.*
4. **Format the Rectangle:** *Change the Format Fill Transparency to 100%.*
5. *The result will look similar to the following:*

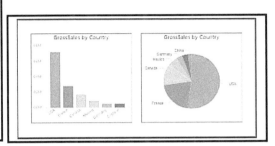

1.56 Image

 **Images** can be added to enhance the look of **Visual Reports**.

Practice Exercise 24 - Image

Images can be added to enhance the look of **Visual Reports**.

In **Power BI Desktop:** *Insert Ribbon Tab →Elements Group →* Image →
C:\Data\PowerBI-2\Background.png.

1.57 Add A Sparkline

This is a different type of **Chart** stored in a **Table Visual**. It will provide help in understanding trends of data by displaying a small **Chart**. A new **Sparkline** option will appear in the **Table Format Pane**.

Practice Exercise 25 - Sparkline Line

Here, we will create a **Table Visual** and **Add A Sparkline..**
1. *Click in the white work area to create a new report.*

2. **Create a Table:** *Select the* ⊞ *Table icon.*
3. **Drag Fields:** *Drag Fields to the Columns Bucket position:*

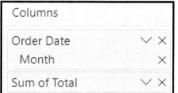

Tip: Be sure to set the **Total** field to **Sum** as shown above (Sum of Total).

4. **Add Sparkline:** *Select the Table →Insert Ribbon Tab →Sparkline Group →*

Add A Sparkline:

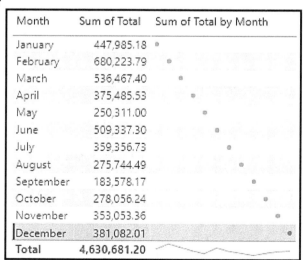

5. *The result is as follows:*

Month	Sum of Total	Sum of Total by Month
January	447,985.18	
February	680,223.79	
March	536,467.40	
April	375,485.53	
May	250,311.00	
June	509,337.30	
July	359,356.73	
August	275,744.49	
September	183,578.17	
October	278,056.24	
November	353,053.36	
December	381,082.01	
Total	4,630,681.20	

6. **Test It:** *Sort the table by pressing the ▲ under the Sum of Mfg Price label.*

Total	4,630,681.20	

Section 5 - Report View / Modeling Ribbon Tab

This will provide an advanced option for establishing relationships between tables and **DAX** programming capabilities.

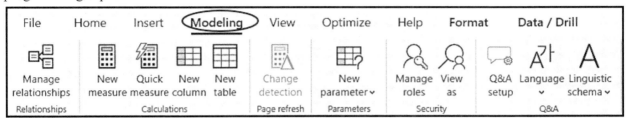

Section Table Of Contents

Practice Exercise 26 - Open BikeDB-B

1. **Open Data Source:** In **Power BI Desktop**→*File Tab*→*Open Report*→*Browse Report*→ *C:\Data\PowerBI-2\BikeDB-B.pbix*→ Open button.
   This will open a **Power BI** file containing the following **Visual Reports**:

Each **Power BI** file will open a new instance of **Power BI** program into memory.

2. **Exit:** To close the above file, you must exit out of **Power BI** completely. *Press the* ❌ *in the upper right corner of the interface.*

1.58 Manage Relationships

This will open Model View and display tables to be related. You will be able to view **Defined**, add **New, Autodetect, Edit,** and **Delete Relationships**.

In the Report View: *Modeling Ribbon Tab*→*Relationships Group*→ *Manage Relationships*.

Tip: This will be discussed in greater detail in Power BI Desktop Workbook - Chapter 7 (Relationships).

1.59 New Measure

A **New Measure** is a calculated summarization of a field located in a **Field List** (on the right side of the interface). This field does not get added to ⊞ **Table View** as a **New Column** but can be used to create a **Visual Report** or be used in another **Measure**. If you want to place calculated results in a new field, use a **New Column**.

Tip: DAX (Data Analysis Expressions) formulas are the programming languages used to define **Measures**. The following is an example of **DAX** formulas:

f_x | Count of Last Year's Sales:=COUNTA([Last Year's Sales])

Tip: Measure results can be placed in a **Visual Report** and are called 🔢 **Cards**.

Practice Exercise 27 - New Measure Adj LYS

1. **Create New Measure:** *In* ⊞ *Table View→Select any field in the Customer Table (located in the Field List)→Home Ribbon Tab →* 🔲 *New Measure.*

2. **Type the Formula:** *Enter the following in the Customer Table:*

   ✕ ✓ | Adj LYS = SUM(Customer[Last Year's Sales]) * 1.2 → ☑ *Commit.*

3. **Create A Card:** Drag a **Measure** to the work area in order to create a **Visual Report**. The default **Visual Report** should be a **Card**-style **Visual Report**.

   Tip: The **Measure is** located in the **Field List** (located on the right-side of the interface) and can be used to create a new **Visual Report**.

   3.23M

   Adj LYS

Practice Exercise 28 - New Measure Sum Of Total

Create a **Measure** in a **Power BI interface:**

Tip: Make sure you have the **Orders** table selected in the **Field List.**

1. **Select the Orders Table:** *Select the Orders Table in the Field List to make sure the Measure created will get stored in the proper place.*

2. **Create a New Measure:** *In the* 📊 *Report View →Modeling Ribbon Tab → Calculations Group →* 🔲 *New Measure.*

3. **Type the formula:** *Type in the following in the Orders Table:*

   ✕ ✓ | Sum of Total = SUM(Orders[Total]) → ☑ *Commit.*

4. **Go To Report View:** *Switch to* 📊 *Report View.*

5. **Create A Card Visual:** *Place the Measure in a Card Visual Report→ Click the* 🔢 *Card Visual→Drag n Drop the "Sum of Total" Measure to the Card Visual.*

6. *The end result should look similar to the following:*

   4.63M

   Sum of Total

1.60 Quick Measure

You can use [icon] **Quick Measures** to quickly and easily create common, powerful calculations. **Quick Measure** opens a dialog box, you choose the options, then it creates a **New Measure** to be used in your report.
Refer to the **New Quick Measure** capability located in: <u>Chapter 3 Sections 5</u>.

1.61 New Column

[icon] This will create a [icon] **New Column** in the [icon] **Table View** layout and can be used to combine several fields into one [icon] **New Column,** calculate several numeric fields into the [icon] **New Column,** or perform a mathematical operation of a field. The formulas in the [icon] **New Column** are much like the formulas created in **Measures.** You can also create [icon] **New Columns** that are based on **Measures** and other **New Columns.** However, avoid using the same name for [icon] **New Columns** and **Measures,** as this can lead to confusing results. The **New Column** will be added to the **Field List** and will appear as a new field in [icon] **Table View.** They are often referred to as calculated fields. The following are a few examples of [icon] **New Columns:**

```
Column = [Country] & [Product]
```
```
NewColumn=[FirstName] & " " & [LastName]
```
```
Total Sales = [Sale Price] * [Units]
```

Practice Exercise 29 - New Column Location

1. **Create a New Column:** *In the* [icon] *Report View →Modeling Ribbon Tab →Calculations Group →* [icon] *New Column →Enter the following in the Customer Table:*
```
Location = [City] & ", " & [Region] & ", " & [Country]
```
→ ☑ Commit.

2. *Review the New Column in the Field List located on the left side of the interface. The* [icon] *Table View is located on the right side of the interface.*

1.62 New Table

[icon] This will allow you to create a **New Table** that is referenced to another existing **Table.** The advantage of a reference **Table** (as opposed to copying / duplicating the **Table**) is that when the primary table is adjusted, the new table will also be adjusted.

Practice Exercise 30 - New Table

In the [icon] **Report View:** *Modeling Ribbon Tab →Calculations Group →* [icon] *New Table icon →enter the following:*
```
Table = Products
```
→ ☑ Commit.
Review the table in the field list located on the right side of the interface.

1.63 Change Detection

This is a **Power BI Premium** feature that will automatically refresh a report only when a change is detected. However, if a data source is extremely large, a regular refresh may slow things down. Currently, this function is disabled in **Power BI Pro Web Service**.

1.64 New Parameter

This feature creates a custom **Slicer** that can be applied to a **Measure**. The **Measure** is a calculated formula that can be applied to a **Chart**. It will allow you to adjust a **Slicer Parameter** to see a **What-If** scenario.

1. Create a **What-if parameter:**

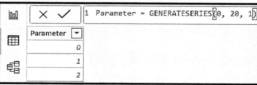

2. **Field List:** The result of the **Parameter** automatically creates a **Table** and a **Measure**.

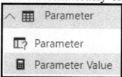

3. **Parameter Table:** The **Parameter** creates a **Parameter Table** that enters the numeric range specified in the **Parameter**.
4. **Measure:** Next, use a **Parameter Value** to create a **Measure**.
5. **Chart:** Then, apply the measure to a **Chart**.

Tip: This capability will be discussed in more detail in the **DAX Programming** workbook because it involves **Measures** and **Custom Tables**.

Practice Exercise 31 - New Parameter

The **Discount Amt** is the discount applied to each country. The maximum discount percent is about **15%**. Calculate the average discount applied to each company.

1. **Create a New Parameter using the values from 0% to 15%: In the** **Report View:**

Modeling Ribbon Tab→What IF Group→ New Parameter→*Enter the following:*

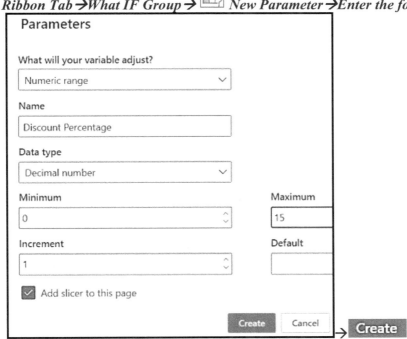

2. *Create a Measure to apply Parameter results to the Sum of the Total:*

Home Ribbon Tab→Calculations Group→ New Measure→*Enter the following:*

```
Total Discount = SUM(Orders[Total]) * [Discount Percentage Value]/100
```

3. *Change the Slider to 15:*

4. *Create a* *Clustered Column Chart→*

5. **Test It:** *As you move the slider, you can see the average discount applied to each country.*

1.65 Manage Roles

Power BI uses a **Role-Based** security model that includes defining a **Role** and then assigning users to that **Role**. However, within that **Role**, you can restrict or allow users to see specific rows within a **Table** by using a **DAX** expression. For example, if I want the **USA** team to see only their data, then I would create a **Role** that uses a **DAX** filter on the **Table** that defines only the **USA**. This will **Filter** the **Table** in your model to specifically display **USA** data.

Tip: Refer to _Power BI Pro Web Workbook - Chapter 2 Section 1 (Security)_ for more details on **Manage Roles**.

1.66 View As Roles

This will allow you to **View Roles** that have been established in **Power BI Desktop**. **Tip:** Refer to _Power BI Pro Web Workbook - Chapter 2 Section 1 Student Project B2 (View As Roles)_ for more details on **Manage Roles**.

1.67 Q&A Setup

This will open a setup dialog box for the **Questions** and **Answers** feature.

Tip: This feature will be covered in greater detail in _Power BI Web Pro Workbook - Chapter 4 Section 4 (Ask A Question)_.

1.68 Language

This will establish the **Language** used:

✓	English
	Spanish [Preview]

1.69 Linguistic Schema

This is used in conjunction with the **Q&A** feature. It will allow you to import a predefined phrase in order to predict what people will be typing. You can also add alternative words in the **Synonyms Pane**.

Section 6 - Connection Techniques

This will discuss the different ways to get data from a data source.

Section Table Of Contents

1.70 Import

This will extract data and store it into a **Power BI Data Set**. When you press the refresh button, new data will be extracted from the master data base and update the **Power BI Data Set.** The **Power BI** standard version has a size limitation of 1 Gb and the **Power BI Premium** is 10Gb. The size limitation may change, but if you own your own server, it can be adjusted. Most **Get Data** connection types will support this **Import** feature. One main advantage is speed. Since data is cached in memory, you don't need to pull data from a storage location. The disadvantage is the size limitations discussed above.

1.71 Direct Query

This will extract the schema or Model (relationships) structure, the data will remain live. You won't need to do a refresh because new data will be loaded directly and automatically. **Model View** will display the structure and relationships between tables. One disadvantage is there could be speed problems between **Power BI** and the actual data storage. However, if you have **Power BI Cache** limitation, this may be an option. Not all connection types are supported.

1.72 Live Connection

This will allow you to connect to an Analysis service or a **Power BI Data Set**. No data will be cached in the **Power BI** and data will be displayed live as it changes at the source. There will be no **Model View** and all changes to a **Data Model** must be made at the source.

1.73 Composite Models

The latest version of **Power BI** allow you to designate tables as Import and **Direct Query**. You would first import all tables and, in the **Model View,** refefine them using table **Properties**. You should also consider using the **Perfromance Analyze**r to monitor performance.

Chapter 2 - Query Editor

The **Query Editor** interface will allow users to link to data sources such as **Excel, CSV, XML, Text, SQL Server, Access, Oracle, MySQL, SharePoint List, Active Directory,** websites across the enterprise, and **Facebook**. Linking to a data source can also be done in the **Power BI Desktop** interface using the **Get Data** command. Once a data source is linked to the **Query Editor** interface, you can reduce the amount of data available for **Reports** or remove unnecessary fields. Also, there are many customized techniques used to adjust data including adjusting columns(fields), rows (records), split columns, combine columns, replace information, transpose an entire table, change the **Data Type**, and sort columns. The **Query Editor** is used to filter, transform, or shape data source information and each **Query** adjustment is saved by name. Information can then be easily removed in the **Applied Steps Query Settings**. Also, you can return to the **Query Editor** at any time to make additional adjustments as necessary. When finished, the resulting data can be saved to **Power BI** and results can be previewed in ⊞ **Table View**.

Chapter Table of Contents

Section 1 - Query Editor Interface

The interface above is the **Query Editor** interface used to manipulate a data source. At this point, you can filter or eliminate undesired records. If you pull data from an information website (such as government census data), you will need to reduce the amount of information coming into **Power BI**. The goal of this step is to shape or adjust the amount of information flowing into **Power BI Desktop**. This is helpful in order to reduce the amount and overall size of information for creating reports.

Section Table Of Contents

Practice Exercise 32 - Get Data QAccounting1

Power BI Procedure:

1. **Begin a new blank Report:** *Start Power BI Desktop or a new blank report (File Tab →* New *New).*

2. ⊞ **Get Data Source:** *Home Ribbon Tab →Data Group →* ⊞ *Get Data dropdown arrow →*

    ⊞ *Excel Workbook →C:\Data\PowerBI-2\QAccounting1.xlsx →* `Open` *button.*

3. **Select an Excel Sheet:** *Choose the Accounting Sheet.*

Display Options ▾

    ▲ 🖿 AccountingB.xlsx

      ☑ ⊞ Accounting

      ☐ ⊞ Sheet1

      ☐ ⊞ Sheet2 → `Transform Data` *button.*

    Tip: To **Exit** the **Query Editor,** press ⊞ **Close & Apply.**

2.1 Get Data

⊞ Often, a data source is located outside of **Power BI** (**External** data source). However, **Get Data** will maintain a connection to the data source and a **Refresh** will bring in any new or updated information from that data source into **Power BI**. This is the first step in the process and supports many data sources for **Power BI Desktop**.

In Power BI Desktop: *Home Ribbon Tab →Data Group →* ⊞ *Get Data dropdown arrow →*

⊞ *Excel Workbook*.

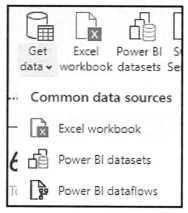

2.2 Data Source

You can connect to a variety of **Sources** such as local small databases, larger server-based databases, and data warehouses. A data warehouse is a special type of database that is a storage collection of information which is not usually actively updated. Also, data can be extracted from websites such as government census, **Linkedin, Facebook** data, etc. Some of the more common **Data Sources** include **Excel, Access, SQL, Oracle, SAP, etc.**

2.3 Load

This will **Import** all data directly to **Power BI** and a **Refresh** will bring in any new or updated information from the data source into **Power BI**. Then, it will skip to the **Filter/Query** (**Transform Data**) step and **Load** data into **Power BI** in order to build **Visual Reports**.

Tip: A **Refresh** will bring in any new or updated information from a data source into **Power BI**.

2.4 Transform Data

This will open the **Power Query Editor** to filter or transform incoming data by reducing or adjusting information. For example, you might have one million records or 20 years of data and the **Query Editor** will allow you to select specific records needed. To open the **Query Editor**, choose the

Transform button. To relaunch the **Query Editor** after you choose ⬛ **Close & Apply**: *Choose* 📊

Report View→ Home Ribbon Tab →Queries Group → 📋*Transform data*.

When finished making changes, choose ⬛ **Close & Apply** to save the resulting query to **Power BI Desktop**.

2.5 Sort

By pressing the dropdown arrow, you can sort the column alphabetically.

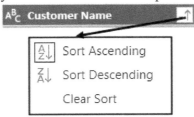

2.6 Filter

The **Query Editor** interface is used to manipulate a data source by applying **Filters** and eliminate undesired records. If you pull data from an information website (such as government census data), you will need to reduce the amount of information coming into **Power BI**. This works similar to the **Excel Filter** feature that filters records in a worksheet.

▦ ▾	1²₃ Customer ID	▾	Aᴮ_C Customer Name	▾	Aᴮ_C Market	▾	Aᴮ_C Country	▾	Aᴮ_C Discount
1	1		City Cyclists		Large		USA		None
2	2		Pathfinders		Medium		USA		None
3	3		Bike-A-Holics Anonymous		Small Business		USA		None
4	13		C-Gate Cycle Shoppe		Small Business		USA		None

Tip: Press the down arrow on top of each column to filter or **Load** specific records to **Power BI**.

2.7 Left Pane

The **Left Pane** displays the number of active queries as well as the name of a **Table/Sheet**. When you select a **Query** from the **Left Pane** (see screen capture in the beginning of the chapter), its data will be displayed in the **Center Pane**.

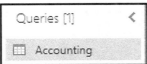

Tip: This is usually the original data source **Table** name. However, it is sometimes referred to as a **Query** because when it is filtered, it becomes a subset of the original **Table**. This chapter will refer

to the **Query** name (above) as an **Excel Worksheet**, **Excel Table**, **Query**, or **Table/Query** interchangeably.

2.8 Center Pane

In the **Center Pane**, the data, or result of the selected **Query** is displayed. This is where filtering results are accomplished. Filters can also be applied to **Fields/Columns**, and when filtered then become a subset of the original **Table**.

⊞▾	1²₃ Customer ID	▾	Aᴮ_C Customer Name	▾	Aᴮ_C Market	▾	Aᴮ_C Cour
1	1		City Cyclists		Large		USA
2	2		Pathfinders		Medium		USA
3	3		Bike-A-Holics Anonymous		Small Business		USA
4	13		C-Gate Cycle Shoppe		Small Business		USA
5	14		Alley Cat Cycles		Midmarket		USA

Tip: Data contained in **Power BI Desktop** is the output of the **Query Editor** as a **Data Table**. However, it can also be called a filter, transformed data, or shape data. Also, the words **Query** and **Table** are used interchangeably in this document.

Practice Exercise 33 - Filter

> **Filter** the **Market Field/Column** name to **Large** only.
> Continue from the previous practice exercise.
> 1. **In the Power Query Editor:** *Click the down arrow in the Market field* ▾.
> 2. *Uncheck Select All* ☐ (Select All).
> 3. *Check Large* ☑ Large → **OK**.

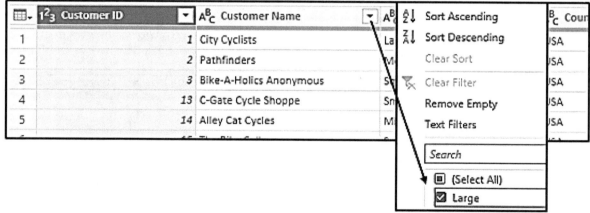

> 4. *Review the results below:*

⊞▾	1²₃ Customer ID	▾	Aᴮ_C Customer Name	▾	Aᴮ_C Market	▾↑	Aᴮ_C Country
1	202		Sunrise Cycle		Large		England
2	36		Road Runners Paradise		Large		USA
3	16		Hercules Mountain Bikes		Large		USA
4	232		Fast Mover Pte Ltd		Large		China
5	111		Bikefest		Large		USA
6	76		Canal City Cycle		Large		Canada
7	121		Caledonia Cycle		Large		USA
8	116		Colin's Bikes		Large		USA
9	26		Blazing Saddles		Large		USA

2.9 Properties

Properties are located on the right side of an interface. Included within **Properties** is the **Table/Sheet Name** which can be renamed if necessary.

2.10 Applied Steps

Whenever you add a **Query** step or filter to **Power Query Editor,** it is inserted into the sequence of steps located in the **Query Settings/Applied Steps**. Usually, steps are added at the end of a sequence, but if you add a step anywhere other than at the end of the flow, you should verify that all subsequent steps function properly. For instance, if you remove a column in the **Query Editor,** the filter setting will be stored in the **Applied Settings** area. If a filter needs to be removed from the **Query Setting Pane**, simply delete the filter desired.

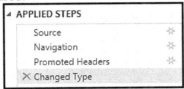

Practice Exercise 34 - Remove Applied Steps

Create and **Remove** a record from the **Applied Steps** of **Filtered Rows**.

1. **Create a Filtered Row:** *Click the down arrow in the Country field* ⌄ → *Uncheck Select All* ☐ (Select All) →*Check Canada* ☑ Canada → OK .

2. **Remove Applied Steps:** *To remove the Applied Steps, press the* ☒ *in the following:*

   ☒ Filtered Rows

3. **Exit Query Editor:** To Exit the **Query Editor,** press 🗙 **Close & Apply.**

2.11 Group Queries

If you have multiple **Queries** (located on the left side of the **Query Editor**), you can group them for organizational purposes. For example, if you created a query from an **SQL** statement, these can be moved to an **SQL Group** and regular **Tables** can be moved into a different **Group**.

Practice Exercise 35 - Query Group

To create a New Group: *In Power BI →Home Ribbon Tab →Queries Group →*🖾*Transform Data →Right-Click in the Gray area under the query names (located on the left side of the interface) →New Group →Name: MyGroup.*
To move a Query to the New Group: *Right-Click on any table →Move to Group →My Group.*

Section 2 - Query Editor / Home Ribbon Tab

The **Home Ribbon Tab** provides the most commonly used features which will be covered in this section:

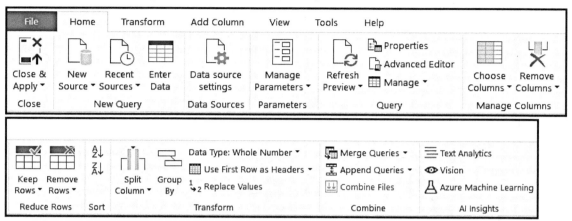

Section Table Of Contents

Practice Exercise 36 - Get Data QAccounting1

1. **Begin a new blank Report:** *Start Power BI Desktop or a new blank report (File Tab →* New *New).*

2. Get Data Source: In Power BI Desktop: *Home Ribbon Tab→Data Group →* Get Data *dropdown arrow→* Excel Workbook →*C:\Data\PowerBI-2\QAccounting1.xlsx →* Open *button.*

3. **Select Sheet:** *Choose the Accounting Sheet:*

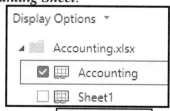

4. **Transform Data in the Query Editor:** Transform Data *button.* This will open the **Query Editor** in order to adjust or filter data.

Queries [1]								Query Settings	×
Accounting	▦▾	1²₃ Customer ID ▾	Aᴮ𝒸 Customer Name ▾	Aᴮ𝒸 Market ▾	Aᴮ𝒸 Country ▾	Aᴮ𝒸 D		◢ PROPERTIES	
	1	1	City Cyclists	Large	USA	Nc		Name	
	2	2	Pathfinders	Medium	USA	Nc		Accounting	
	3	3	Bike-A-Holics Anonymous	Small Business	USA	Nc		All Properties	
	4	13	C-Gate Cycle Shoppe	Small Business	USA	Nc		◢ APPLIED STEPS	
	5	14	Alley Cat Cycles	Midmarket	USA	Nc		Source	⇎
	6	15	The Bike Cellar	Small	USA	Nc		Navigation	⇎
	7	16	Hercules Mountain Bikes	Large	USA	Nc		Promoted Headers	⇎
	8	17	Whistler Rentals	Medium	USA	Nc		✕ Changed Type	
	9	28	Pedals Inc.	Small Business	USA	Nc			

fx = Table.TransformColumnTypes(#"Promoted Headers",{{"Customer ID", Int64.Type},

2.12 Close & Apply

When finished manipulating the **Query,** choose the "**Close and Apply" button**. The filtering defined in the **Query** will be **Applied** to the **Data Table** in **Power BI** to be used for a **Visual Report**. You can open the **Query Editor** at any time and reapply or filter new records.

> Close & Apply
> Apply
> Close

Practice Exercise 37 - Close And Apply

1. **Close the Query Editor:** If the **Query Editor** is open, press ⬚ **Close&Apply**.
2. **Open the Query Editor:** If you are at the **Power BI** interface in **Power BI:** *Home Ribbon Tab → Queries Group →* ⬚ *Transform Data dropdown arrow →* ⬚ *Transform Data*.

2.13 New Source

You can connect to a variety of **Sources** such as local, small databases, larger server-based databases, and data warehouses. A data warehouse is a special type of database that has a storage collection of information usually not actively updated. Also, data can be extracted from websites such as a government census, **LinkedIn** data, etc. Some of the more common **Data Sources** include **Excel, SQL, Access**, etc. **Tip:** This can also be done in **Power BI Desktop** using the **Get Data** command.

Practice Exercise 38 - New Source

1. **Open New Data Source:** In Power Query Editor: *Home Ribbon Tab → New Query Group →* ⬚ *New Source → More . . . →* ⬚ *Access Database →* `Connect` *→ C:\Data\PowerBI-2\Northwind 2008.accdb →* `Open` *button.*
   Tip: If you receive an "**Unable to Connect**" error, this is because **Access** is installed as a 32-bit installation and **Power BI** is installed as 64-bit.
2. **Select Table:** *Choose the Customers Table.*

This will get the **Data Source** and place it in the **Query Editor**.

Tip: The other way to load a file is: In **Power BI Desktop:** *Home Ribbon Tab→Data Group→* *Get Data dropdown arrow→More…→* *Access Database→* *Connect button→* *C:\Data\PowerBI-2\Northwind 2008.accdb→* *Open* *→Choose the ✔ Customers Table→* Transform Data *button.*

2.14 Recent Sources

 After you have opened a **Data Source**, its name will be listed under the **Recent Sources** button. This is a shortcut to the previously accessed **Data Source**.
In Power Query Editor→Home Ribbon Tab→New Query Group→ 🕓 *Recent Sources.*

Most Recent	
A📇	Northwind 2008.accdb
X📇	Accounting.xlsx

2.15 Enter Data

This will create a new blank **Table** and will allow you to enter new data.
Tip: Another technique used to create a new table in **Power BI Desktop** is the *Home Ribbon Tab →* *New Table command.*
To create a **Table** based on another **Table: In Power BI:** Choose *Modeling Ribbon Tab →Calculations Group →New Table.*

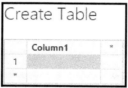

Create Table

	Column1	※
1		
※		

Practice Exercise 39 - Enter Data

Create a new **Table** and **Enter Data**.

1. **Enter Data:** *In Power Query Editor→Home Ribbon Tab →New Query Group →Enter Data→ Enter values 1 through 20→ Name: Table1→* OK .

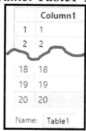

	Column1
1	1
2	2
18	18
19	19
20	20
Name:	Table1

Tip: The new **Query**, called **Table1**, will be located on the left side of the interface.

2.16 Data Source Settings

This will allow you to change the physical location of a **Data Source** to a different **Source** location containing similar data records. It can be used to point to a previous backup or a newer **Data**

Source of information. Once a **Data Source** is defined, the previously developed **Visual Reports** can display this new information. Also, you can change the permissions to **None, Public, Organizational**, or **Private** rights in order to restrict access when defining multiple **Data Sources.**

In Power Query Editor: *Home Ribbon Tab→Data Sources Group→* ⬚ *Data Source Settings or*

In Power Query Editor: *File Tab→* ⬚ *Options and Settings →Data Source Settings.*

The three options above will be reviewed below:

2.16a Change Source [Change Source...] - This will allow you to change the location of a source or a different source that contains a similar structure. It may be a backup or a historical data source.

⬚ *Data Source Settings →Change Source* [Change Source...] .

> **Excel Workbook**
>
> • Basic   ○ Advanced
>
> File path
> C:\Data\PowerBI-1\QAccounting1.xlsx   [Browse...]
>
> Open file as
> Excel Workbook ▾

2.16b ⬚ **Export PBIDS**

In **October of 2019, Power BI** released a new file type with a file extension of **.PBIDS**. The **Power BI Desktop Source (PBIDS)** file is a **JSON** object file used to store information to connect **Data Sources, Templates**, and **Themes**. If a new user starts **Power BI** by using this file, a data connection will be automatically built in. It won't be necessary to use the **Get Data** command in order to connect to a **Data Source**. All that is needed is to open the file, enter login credentials to the **Data Source**, and select all desired tables in the navigation dialog box. To create a **PBIDS** file from an existing report, choose the **Export PBIDS** option.

> **In Power BI Query Editor:** *Home Ribbon Tab →Data Sources Group→* ⬚ *Data Source Settings →Export PBIDS.*

2.16c Edit Permissions - This will allow you to edit or change the **Sensitivity** or **Privacy Levels** that can be used to block or isolate different **Data Sources** from each other. **Note**: This may reduce functionality and impact performance.

> **Tip**: The **May 2021 Update** added new **Sensitivity Levels** to enhance **Security** and give more control to businesses/users.

> **Tip**: The **Aug 2021 Update** allows an **Administrator** to set the **System Default Sensitivity Levels** even though a user can redefine them to override **Administrator Defaults**.

⚙ **Data Source Settings→Edit Permissions** [Edit Permissions...] .

Edit Permissions

☐ c:\data\powerbi-2\financial sample2.xlsx

Privacy Level

None	▼
None	
Public	OK
Organizational	
Private	

Private - Use this feature if a **Data Source** contains sensitive or confidential information. The visibility of a **Data Source** may be restricted to authorized users only and will be isolated from other **Data Sources**. An example might be if you were connecting to a specific **Facebook** account or a **Data Source** containing employee payroll information.

Organizational - Use this **Data Source** to limit visibility to a trusted group of people only. An example might be if you were accessing a file located on an intranet **SharePoint** site with permissions enabled for a trusted group only.

Public - This gives everyone visibility rights to data contained in the **Data Source**. However, only files on the internet **Data Sources** or workbooks can be marked **Public**.

None - This is the default setting if privacy levels are not needed.

2.16d Clear Permissions [Clear Permissions ▼] - This will remove all permission settings back to **None** or to the Administrator's defaults.

Clear Permissions

Clear All Permissions

2.16e Global Permissions [⦿ Global permissions] - This will allow you to change a **Data Source** to a different internet-based **Data Source** such as **LinkedIn**.

○ Data sources in current workbook   ⦿ Global permissions

Another use of **Parameters** is to change **Data Source Settings** in **Dashboards** and **Reports**. These parameters are more flexible than the **Filter** capacity because it is easy to change in **Power BI Desktop**. **Tip**: As of now, **Parameters** can only be added to data model queries in the **Power BI Desktop**. However, this functionality is NOT available when using **Power BI Pro Web Service** (It may be available in future versions).

Practice Exercise 40 - Change Source

1. **Begin a new blank Report:** *Start Power BI Desktop or a new blank report (File Tab →* [New] *New).*

2. 🗇 **Get Data Source: In Power BI Desktop:** *Home Ribbon Tab→Data Group →* 🗇*Get Data dropdown arrow →* 🗎 *Excel Workbook →C:\Data\PowerBI-2\QAccounting1.xlsx →* [Open] *button→Choose the Accounting Sheet →* [Transform Data] *button.*

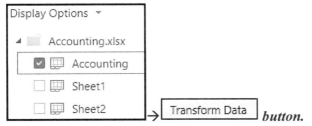 *button.*

3. **Change Data Source:** *In Power Query Editor→Home Ribbon Tab→Data Sources Group→*  *Data Source Settings→Select QAccounting1.xlsx→Change Source* *(located at the bottom of the Data Source Settings dialog box.*

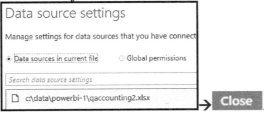

4. **Find New Data Source:** *Browse to find the new data source.*

5. *The result is the Data Source will look the same, but there could be more or fewer records available. In Power Query Editor→Home Ribbon Tab→Data Sources Group→*  *Data Source Settings.*

2.17 Manage Parameters

This could be used in conjunction with an **SQL Query** in order to provide an answer to a **SQL** statement when a record or group of records is needed. It can also be used to provide a value to be used in a filter.

> Manage Parameters
> Edit Parameters
> New Parameter

Manage Parameters - This involves adjusting the properties of a previously created **Parameter**.
Edit Parameters - This provides a method of adjusting a **Parameter** data value used.
New Parameter - This involves adding a new **Parameter** to all queries.

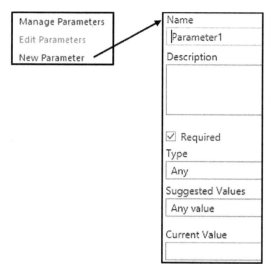

Tip: In order to remove a **Parameter** definition, you must remove the **Filter** from the **Query** (see practice exercise 42- Delete Parameters). Then, you will be able to delete the defined parameter

(see *In Power Query Editor→Home Ribbon Tab→ Parameters Group→**Manage Parameters dropdown→Manage Parameters*).

Practice Exercise 41 - Manage Parameters

1. **Select Table:** *In Power Query Editor→Select Accounting Query*.

2. **New Parameter:** *Home Ribbon Tab→Parameters Group→ Manage Parameters → New Parameter*.

3. **Enter Parameter Information:** *Enter the following information, then press* **OK**.

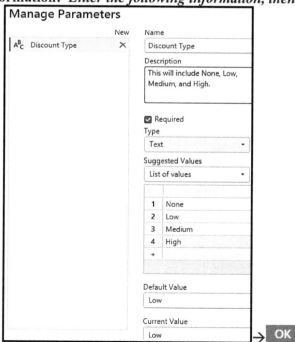

4. **Apply a Filter**: *Select Accounting Query →Select Discount Type field → Filter dropdown arrow→Text Filters→Equals*.

5. **Apply the Parameter to the Filter:** *Choose the Parameter option in the dropdown arrow.*
   See the **Filter** dialog box below:

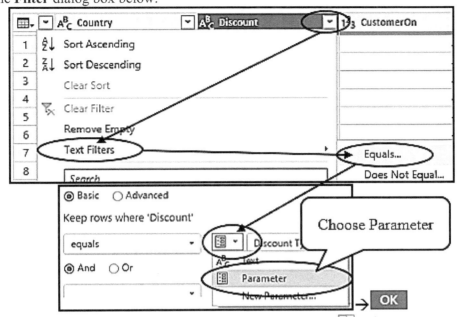

6. **In Power Query Editor:** *Home Ribbon Tab →Query Group →* ⬚ *Refresh Preview dropdown →* ⬚ *Refresh All.*

7. *The results is it will look similar to the following:*

⊞▾	1²₃ Customer ID	A⁸c Customer Name	A⁸c Market	A⁸c Country	A⁸c Discount	1²₃ C
1	60	Bikes for Tykes	Small	Canada	Low	
2	79	Helsinki Bicycle	Midmarket	France	Low	
3	80	France Sports	Small	France	Low	
4	81	Centre Sportif Cherbourg	Large	France	Low	
5	82	Vélos Basse Normandie	Medium	France	Low	
6	83	Calais Cyclisme	Small Business	France	Low	

8. **Test It:** *In Power Query Editor→Home Ribbon Tab →Parameters Group →* ⬚ *Manage Parameters dropdown arrow→Edit Parameter → (Change the parameter value to Medium) →* OK .

Refresh:
   Tip: You may need to do a **Refresh:** *In Power Query Editor →Home Ribbon Tab → Query Group →* ⬚ *Refresh Preview.*

9. **In Power Query Editor:** *Home Ribbon Tab →Query Group →* ⬚ *Refresh Preview dropdown →* ⬚ *Refresh All.*

⊞▾	1²₃ Customer ID	A⁸c Customer Name	A⁸c Market	A⁸c Country	A⁸c Discount
1	220	Wheels 'n' Deals	Midmarket	Canada	Medium
2	221	Halifax Cycle Centre	Small	Canada	Medium
3	222	Dag City Cycle	Large	Canada	Medium

Tip: You can also modify a parameter directly: Select the **Discount Type Query** on the left side of the interface.

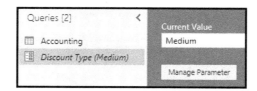

Practice Exercise 42 - Delete Parameters

1. **Clear the Parameter Filter:** *In Power Query Editor→Select the Filter dropdown arrow* ⬇*in the Discount Field →Clear Filter* 🔻 Clear Filter .

2. **Delete Parameter:** *Home Ribbon Tab → Parameters Group→*▦*Manage Parameter dropdown arrow→Manage Parameter→Press the* ☒ *to delete the Discount Type:*

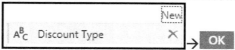

3. **Refresh All:** *Home Ribbon Tab →Query Group →*▤*Refresh Preview dropdown arrow →* ▤*Refresh All.* **Tip:** If it doesn't **Refresh,** try to **Refresh** again.

Practice Exercise 43 - Manage Data Source

1. **Select Table:** *In Power Query Editor→Select Accounting Table.*

2. **New Parameter:** *Home Ribbon Tab →Parameters Group→*▦ *Manage Parameters→ New Parameter:*

3. **Enter Parameter Information:** *Enter the following information, then press* OK .

4. **Apply a Filter to the Data Source Settings:** *Home Ribbon Tab →Data Sources Group →* 🗎 *Data Source Settings →* Change Source... → OK → Close .

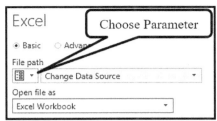

5. **Change the Data Source:** *Select the Change Data Source Query (located on the left side of the interface) →Current Value dropdown arrow: C:\Data\PowerBI-2\QAccounting2.xlsx.*

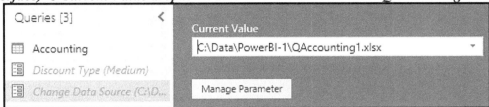

6. **To verify if it is working:** *Home Ribbon Tab → Data Sources Group →* **Data Source Settings**

c:\data\powerbi-1\qaccounting1.xlsx

2.18 Refresh Preview

If a **Data Source** is connected to a live database or connected through a gateway, **Refresh** will **Get New Data** from the **Data Source**.

Refresh Preview - This will only **Refresh** information displayed on a screen.

Refresh Preview
Refresh All
Cancel Refresh

Refresh All - All **Queries/Tables** located on the left side of the screen will be **Refreshed**.

Cancel Refresh - This will allow you to **Cancel** a **Refresh** if it is taking a long time to finish. It may be hung or frozen.

2.19 Properties

 **Properties** are located on the right side of the interface. They contain a **Table/Sheet Name** that can be renamed if necessary.

Name: This will allow you to rename a **Table/Query Name**.

Description: This will allow you to describe the use of this **Table/Query**.

☑ Enable load to report - **Uncheck** this if you want to exclude this specific **Query Name** from being applied **Power BI** when it is refreshed.

☑ Include in report refresh ⓘ - **Uncheck** to this if you want to exclude a **Query Name** from **Refresh**. This may be helpful if a data source is extremely large.

Tip: Checkboxes are usually ☑ **Checked** by default.

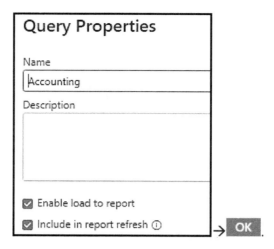

$\rightarrow$ **OK** .

Practice Exercise 44 - Rename

Rename the Accounting Table to **MyAccounting**.
1. **Rename Table:** *Select the Accounting Table →In Power Query Editor →Home Ribbon*

Tab →Query Group → 🔲 *Properties →Name: MyAccounting →* **OK** .

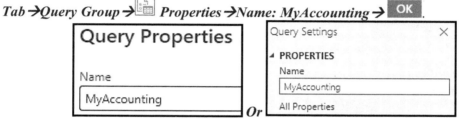

2. **Rename Table:** *Rename the Property Name back to Accounting*.

Tip: A **Table** name can be renamed using the **Query Editor**: *Home Ribbon Tab →Query Group →Properties button,* in the **Query Settings** located on the right side of the interface or **Double-Click** on the **Name** (left side of the interface).

2.20 Advanced Editor

📄 Advanced Editor The **Advanced Editor** is where results of filtering are stored in a text layout. This feature will allow you to view or modify **SQL Code**. These steps are created in the **Query Formula Language**, often referred to as the **M Program Language**.

```
let
    Source = Excel.Workbook(File.Contents("C:\Data\PowerBI-1\QAccounting1.xlsx"), null, true),
    Accounting_Sheet = Source{[Item="Accounting",Kind="Sheet"]}[Data],
    #"Promoted Headers" = Table.PromoteHeaders(Accounting_Sheet, [PromoteAllScalars=true]),
    #"Changed Type" = Table.TransformColumnTypes(#"Promoted Headers",{{"Customer ID", Int64.Type},
        {"Customer Name", type text}, {"Market", type text}, {"Country", type text}, {"Discount",
        type text}, {"CustomerOn", Int64.Type}, {"GrossSales", type number}, {"Discounts", type number},
        {"NetSales", type number}, {"Units", type number}, {"Year", Int64.Type}, {"Month", Int64.Type}})
in
    #"Changed Type"
```

2.21 Manage

⊞ Manage ▾ This will allow you to manipulate a selected **Query** located on the left side of the **Query Editor** interface.

✕	Delete
▤	Duplicate
📎	Reference

Delete - This will **Delete** a selected **Query**.
Duplicate - This makes a copy of a selected **Query**.
Reference - This creates a new **Query** that **References** a selected **Query**.

Practice Exercise 45 - Manage, Delete, Duplicate, And Reference

1. **Duplicate Table:** *Select Accounting Table →Home Ribbon Tab →Query Group→* ▦*Manage →* 📋 *Duplicate.*

2. **Rename:** *Select the Duplicate Table →Home Ribbon Tab →Query Group →* 📑*Properties →* *Name: AccountingDUP →* OK .

3. **Reference Table:** *Select Accounting Table →Home Ribbon Tab →Query Group →* ▦*Manage →* 📎 *Reference.*

4. **Rename:** *Select the Reference Table →Home Ribbon Tab → Query Group →* 📑 *Properties →* *Name: AccountingREF →* OK .

5. **To see how Queries are Referenced:** *View Ribbon Tab →Dependencies Group →* 📑*Query Dependencies:*

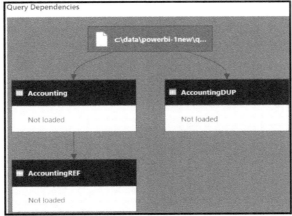

6. **Delete Table:** *Select the Duplicated Query name (located on the left-side of the interface) →*
   In Power Query Editor: *Home Ribbon Tab → Query Group →*▦*Manage →* ✕ *Delete.*
   Tip: *You can also Right-Click on the Duplicate Name →Delete.*

2.22 Choose Columns

▦ This will allow you to add or remove a **Column** by **Checking** or **Unchecking** the ☑ **Checkboxes** next to a specific field. When you ☐ **Uncheck** a field and you choose "**Close and Apply**," the columns will not be available in a **Power BI Desktop Data Table**. In other words, the removed records will be indicated in the **SQL** code as removed. However, records removed in the **Query Editor** are still available in the original data source and can be added back to a **Table** in the **Query Editor** if desired.

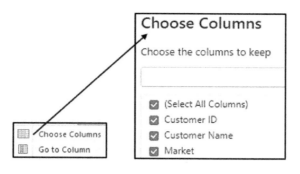

Go To Column - This will find a **Column** located in large **Tables**.
Tip: The **Go To Column** is also available in the *View Ribbon Tab within the Query Editor.*

Practice Exercise 46 - Go To And Choose Column

1. **Select Table:** *In Power Query Editor→Select Accounting Table.*

2. **Move to a Specific Column:** *Home Ribbon Tab→Manage Columns Group→Choose Columns dropdown arrow→ Go To Column→Select the Country Column Name→* OK .

3. **Add/Remove Columns:** *Home Ribbon Tab→Manage Columns Group→Choose Columns dropdown→ Choose Columns→Uncheck the ☐ Country column→* OK .

4. **Select all Columns:** *Home Ribbon Tab→Manage Columns Group→Choose Columns dropdown→ Choose Columns→ ☑ Select All Columns→* OK .

2.23 Remove Columns

Remove Columns
Remove Other Columns

Remove Columns - This **Removes** unwanted selected **Columns**. A **Table** displayed in the **Query Editor** is considered a **Query** because each **Table** might have filters applied to it (located in the **Applied Steps**). **Tip:** You can also **right-click** on a column and choose **Remove Column**.
Remove Other Columns - This will keep selected **Columns** and dispose of the **Other Columns**.
Tip: If a **Column** is used to reference another **Query**, you might receive an error message and will be unable to **Remove** it.

Practice Exercise 47 - Remove Other Columns

1. **Select Table:** *In Power Query Editor→Select Accounting Table (located on the left side of the interface).*

2. **Select Columns:** *Select the desired column(s) to be removed by using the* Ctrl *or* Shift *keys down→Select the Customer Name column.*

3. **Remove Columns:** *In Power Query Editor→Home Ribbon Tab→Manage Columns Group→ Remove Columns dropdown arrow→ Remove Columns.*

4. **Restore Removed Columns:** *On the right side of the Query Editor→* ◢ APPLIED STEPS *→Click the ☒ in the Applied Step* ✕ Removed Columns .

5. **Select Multiple Columns:** *Select desired column(s) you want to keep using the* Ctrl *or* Shift *keys.*

6. **Remove Other Columns:** *In Power Query Editor→Home Ribbon Tab→Manage Columns Group→* *Remove Columns dropdown→* *Remove Other Columns.*

7. **Restore Removed Columns:** *On the right side of the Query Editor→* `◢ APPLIED STEPS` *→Click the* ☒ *in the Applied Step:* `✕ Removed Other Columns`

2.24 Keep Rows

This will **Keep** only specified **Rows** or records. However, other rows in the **Query** will not be displayed. A **Keep Rows** filter is applied to the **Query** in **Applied Steps**. A **Table** displayed in the **Query Editor** is considered a **Query** because each **Table** can have filters applied to it. Each of these **Queries** applied to a **Table** can be removed in the **Applied Steps**.

Keep Top Rows - This will prompt for the number of **Rows** to **Keep**, starting from the row on the **Bottom** of the **Table/Query**.

Keep Bottom Rows - This will prompt for the number of **Rows** to **Keep**, starting from the row on the **Bottom** of the **Query**.

Keep Range of Rows - This will prompt for the range of **Rows** you want to appear in the **Query**.

Keep Duplicates - This will **Keep Duplicates** and remove all other **Rows**.

Keep Errors - This will **Keep** only **Rows** with errors so you can review them.

Practice Exercise 48 - Remove Top Rows

1. **Select Table:** *In Power Query Editor→Select Accounting Table.*

2. **Remove Top Rows:** *Home Ribbon Tab→Reduce Rows Group→* *Keep Rows dropdown arrow→* *Keep Top Rows→Number of rows: 3→* `OK` *.*

Remove Top Rows

Specify how many rows to remove from the top.

Number of rows

3

Only 3 rows will be displayed:

▦▾	1²₃ Customer ID	▾	Aᴮ_C Customer Name	▾	Aᴮ_C Market	▾
1	220		Wheels 'n' Deals		Midmarket	
2	221		Halifax Cycle Centre		Small	
3	222		Dag City Cycle		Large	

3. **Remove the Applied Steps:** *On the right side of the Query Editor→* `◢ APPLIED STEPS` *→Click the* ☒ *in the* `✕ Removed Top Rows` *.*

2.25 Remove Rows

This will **Remove Rows** or records chosen from options available. A **Table** displayed in the **Query Editor** is considered a **Query** due to the filters applied to it. However, each of these **Queries** applied to a **Table,** can be removed in the **Applied Steps**.

	Remove Top Rows
	Remove Bottom Rows
	Remove Alternate Rows
	Remove Duplicates
	Remove Blank Rows
	Remove Errors

Remove Top Rows - This will prompt for the number of **Rows** to **Remove** starting from row 1.

Remove Bottom Rows - This will prompt for the number of **Rows** to be **Removed** beginning from the last record in a data **Query**.

Remove Alternate Rows - To define **Alternate Rows** to **Remove** in a pattern, enter the first **Row** to **Remove**, Number of **Rows** to **Remove**, and Number of **Rows** to **Keep**. (See **practice exercise** below).

Remove Duplicates - This will **Remove** all **Duplicate** records.

Remove Blank Rows - This will **Remove** only **Blank Rows**.

Remove Errors - This will only **Remove Rows** that contain **Errors**.

Practice Exercise 49 - Remove Alternate Rows

Create a new **Table** and **Remove Alternate Rows**:

1. **Create a new blank Table:** *Home Ribbon Tab →New Query Group →* Enter Data *→ Enter values 1 through 20→Name: Table1→* OK .

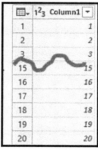

2. **Remove Rows:** *Select Table1 →Home Ribbon Tab →Reduce Rows Group →* Remove Rows *→* Remove Alternate Rows *→Enter the following:*

> **Remove Alternate Rows**
>
> Specify the pattern of rows to remove and keep.
>
> First row to remove
> 5
>
> Number of rows to remove
> 1
>
> Number of rows to keep
> 1

3. **Remove Alternate Rows:** *Delete the filter on the right-side of the interface by Clicking the* ⊠

next to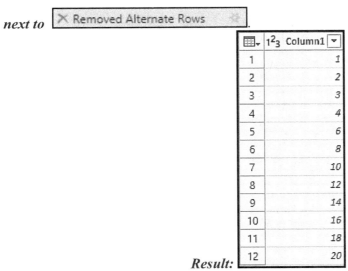

Result:

	1²₃ Column1
1	1
2	2
3	3
4	4
5	6
6	8
7	10
8	12
9	14
10	16
11	18
12	20

4. **Test It:** Type other **Parameters** to test out this feature such as 5 2 1 or 5 2 2 in the **Remove Alternate Rows** dialog box.

5. **Test It:** Use the same **Query** to test out **Remove Top Rows** and **Remove Bottom Rows**.

6. **Remove the Applied Steps:** *On the right side of the Query Editor→* ◢ **APPLIED STEPS** *→Click the* ☒ *in the* ☒ Removed Alternate Rows .

2.26 Sort

⬇ ⬇ This will **Sort** a selected column. **Tip:** This can also be applied by selecting the down arrow located in a column heading.

2.27 Split Column

This will **Split** a **Column** into two columns based on a **Delimitator** character or a specific number of characters. A **Delimitator** is a common identifier character in the middle of a field.

By Delimiter
By Number of Characters

Tip: This feature is also located at: **In Power Query Editor**: *Transform Ribbon Tab→Text Group→* Split Column.

Practice Exercise 50 - Split Column

1. **Select Table:** *In Power Query Editor→Select Accounting Table.*
2. **Select Columns:** *Select two columns using the* Shift *or* Ctrl *keys to select the*

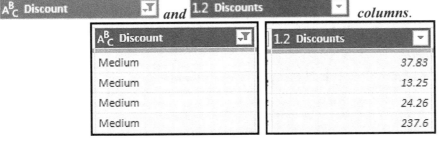

columns.

A♭C Discount	1.2 Discounts
Medium	37.83
Medium	13.25
Medium	24.26
Medium	237.6

3. **Merge two columns:** *Transform Ribbon Tab → Text Column Group →* *Merge Columns.*

Merge Columns

Choose how to merge the selected columns.

Separator

Space

New column name (optional)

Merged

A^BC **Merged**	▼
Medium 37.83	
Medium 13.25	
Medium 24.26	

→ OK

4. **Split Columns:** *Select the Merged column→Home Ribbon Tab →Transform Group →* *Split Column →By Delimiter.*

Split Column by Delimiter

Specify the delimiter used to split the text column.

Select or enter delimiter

Space

Split at

○ Left-most delimiter

○ Right-most delimiter

⦿ Each occurrence of the delimiter

→ OK

5. *The result will look similar to the following:*

A^BC **Merged.1**	▼	1.2 **Merged.2**	▼
Medium		37.83	
Medium		13.25	
Medium		24.26	
Medium		237.6	

6. **Rename the columns to a proper name:** *Double click on the column label →(Enter the following names)*:

ABC 123 Discount Type	▼	ABC 123 Discount Amt	▼
None		579.83	
None		1271.81	
None		1034.81	

2.28 Group By

This will **Group** or summarize all related records in a column and apply a math operation such as counting, summing, etc. Select a column to be grouped, and provide a **New Column Name** as well as the operation to be performed such as Sum, Count, etc. **Tip:** You might want to make a copy of the **Table** because all records in that **Table** will be summarized. *Home Ribbon Tab →Query Group →* *Manage →* *Duplicate.*

The following is the end result of the **Group By Command:**

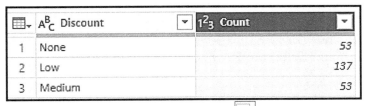

Tip: This is also located in the *Transform Ribbon Tab* ➔ ▣ *Group By*.

Practice Exercise 51 - Group By

1. **Select Table:** *In Power Query Editor* ➔*Select Accounting Table.*
2. **Duplicate Table:** *Home Ribbon Tab* ➔*Query Group* ➔▦*Manage Dropdown* ➔ ▤*Duplicate.*
3. **Group By:** *Open the duplicated Query* ➔*Select the* ᴬᴮC Discount ⊤ *Field* ➔*Home Ribbon Tab* ➔ *Transform Group* ➔▣*Group By.*

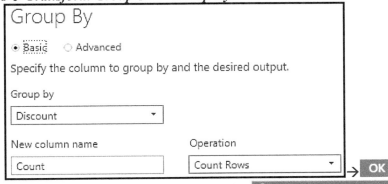

4. *The result will group and count all the records in the* ᴬᴮC Discount ⊤ *field.*

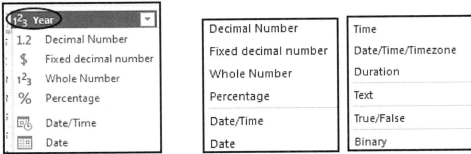

2.29 Data Type

Data Type: This will change a **Data Type** if it was improperly imported into **Power BI**. Tip: Once you learn the **Data Type** symbols, you can change a **Data Type** by selecting the left side of the column label. See Below:

1²₃ Year	Decimal Number	Time
1.2 Decimal Number	Fixed decimal number	Date/Time/Timezone
$ Fixed decimal number	Whole Number	Duration
1²₃ Whole Number	Percentage	Text
% Percentage	Date/Time	True/False
🕒 Date/Time	Date	Binary
▦ Date		

Tip: By default, text fields are left justified and numbers are right-justified. This is a way to visually identify if a **Data Type** is correct.
Tip: This feature is also located at *Transform Ribbon Tab* ➔*Any Column Group* ➔*Data Type.*

Practice Exercise 52 - Data Type

1. **Select Table:** *In Power Query Editor→Select Accounting Table.*
2. **Change the Data Type:** *Select the Month column→Home Ribbon Tab→Transform Group→Data Type dropdown arrow→Text:* | Data Type: Text ▾ | .

Tip: Notice data in the column is now left-justified indicating that it is formatted as a **Text Data Type.** **Tip:** *Also, you can select the* **1.2** *icon in the Month column→Change it to* A^B_C *Text.*

2.30 Use First Row As Headers

If a **Data Source** (or **Get Data**) step did not recognize labels, the **Query Editor** will allow you to define the **First Row As** the **Header** label. Usually, labels will be defined as Column1, Column2, etc., and they will be listed in the **First Row** of data.

	Use First Row as Headers
	Use Headers as First Row

Tip: This feature is also located at: *Transform Ribbon Tab→Table Group→ Use First Row As Headers*.

Practice Exercise 53 - First Row As Headers

1. **New Source:** *In Power Query Editor→Home Ribbon Tab →New Query Group→ New Source→ Excel Workbook→ C:\Data\PowerBI-2\QFirstRowHeader.xlsx→* | Open | *button*.

2. **Choose Table:** *Choose the Product Table.*

Display Options ▾

◢ QFirstRowHeader.xlsx

☑ Product

Product	
Column1	Column2
ProductID	Product
A10011	Beef Hotdog

→ **OK** *button*.

3. **First Row As Headers:** *Home Ribbon Tab→Transform Group→* | Use First Row as Headers ▾ | *dropdown arrow→* | Use First Row as Headers | .

2.31 Replace Value

This is a way to clean up or **Find** and **Replace Values** (or **Data Records**) with different **Values**. A **Value** is any item located anywhere in an entire table.

Tip: This feature is also located at *Transform Ribbon Tab→ Any Column Group→Replace Value.*

Practice Exercise 54 - Replace Values

1. **Select Table:** *In Power Query Editor→Select Accounting Table.*

2. **Replace Values:** *Select the* | A^B_C Country ▾ | *Column→Home Ribbon Tab→ Transform Group→Replace Values→Enter the following parameters.*

Replace Values

Replace one value with another in the selected columns.

Value To Find

A^B_C ▼ | USA

Replace With

A^B_C ▼ | United States

▷ Advanced options

→ OK .

2.32 Merge Queries

This will **Merge** a primary source record with a secondary source. Duplicate records will be replaced, keeping the primary record, and placed into a single new Table. You will need to use the **New Source** command to bring different data sources into the **Query Editor**. The primary data source will be considered first but any new record can be added. Another way to **Merge** records is **Table1** contains product information and **Table2** contains order information. The **Merge Query** will create a single **Query** containing the order information and the product description added to the **Combined Query**.

Merge Queries

Merge Queries as New

Tip: The files must have a similar structure. Additional changes to a **Query** need to be made in the formula editor using **M Code** (however, **M Code** and the editor will not be discussed in this book).

Join Kind: Full Outer Join - This will **Merge** data from two **Tables** into one **Table**. No duplicate records will be **Merged**.

Join Kind: Inter - This will **Merge** only records that match in both **Tables**.

Practice Exercise 55 - Merge Similar Data Source

Customer100 Table has 100 records. **Customer10 Table** has the first 10 records of the **Customer100 Table**. Therefore, the first 10 records are duplicate records.

1. **New Source:** *In Power Query Editor → Home Ribbon Tab →New Query Group →* New

   Source → Excel Workbook *→ C:\Data\PowerBI-*
   2\QMergeQuery.xlsx → Open *button →Select both Tables:*

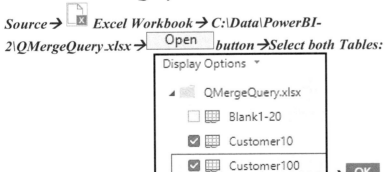

   Display Options ▼

   ◢ QMergeQuery.xlsx
   ☐ Blank1-20
   ☑ Customer10
   ☑ Customer100

   → OK .

2. **Merge Queries:** *In Power Query Editor → Home Ribbon Tab →Combine Group →* Merge

Queries dropdown →  *Merge Queries As New Enter the Merge parameters: Choose Join Kind: Full Outer(all rows from both)* → *Select* OK .

3. *The results will be the first 10 records will not be duplicated but will be replaced with the same Customer ID. If there are unique records in the Customer10 Table, the Customer ID record will be added to the Merged result.*

Practice Exercise 56 - Merge Records

1. **New Source:** *In Power Query Editor → Home Ribbon Tab →New Query Group →* New

   Source → *Excel Workbook → C:\Data\PowerBI-2\BikeDB-B.xlsx →* Open *→Select*

   Sheet Customer and Orders → OK .

2. **Merge Queries:** *In Power Query Editor → Home Ribbon Tab →Combine Group →* Merge

   Queries dropdown arrow → *Merge Queries As New Enter the Merge parameters below*

   then choose OK . *Be sure to select the Customer ID and choose:*

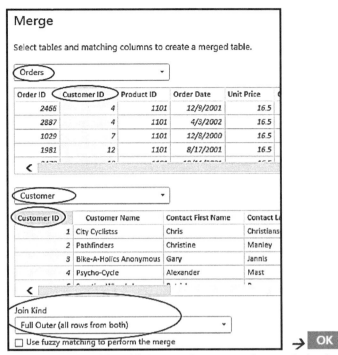

3. **Expand the Customer Table:** This will **Expand** or append records in the **Customer** sheet to each **Orders Record**. *Open the result merge table →Move t the far right of the table → Click on the* ⬍ *icon located on the right side of the* 🔲 Customer ⬍ *Field →Choose* ◉ Expand → OK .

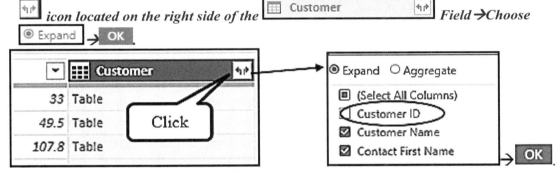

4. The result is the **Customer** records will be added to the **Orders** records:

Shipped	Payment Received	1.2 Total	Customer.Customer Name	
TRUE	TRUE	33	Psycho-Cycle	
TRUE	FALSE	49.5	Psycho-Cycle	
TRUE	TRUE	107.8	Psycho-Cycle	
TRUE	TRUE	269.5	City Cyclistss	
TRUE	TRUE	161.7	City Cyclistss	

2.33 Append Queries

This will allow you to **Append** two **Tables (Queries),** (located on the left side of the interface), into one **Query**. When you **Append** two **Data Source**s into one, the primary **Data Source** will be considered first and any new records can be added.

Append Queries

Append Queries as New

Tip: **Merge** will eliminate duplicates and **Append** will keep duplicates.

Practice Exercise 57 - Append

1. **New Source:** *In Power Query Editor → Home Ribbon Tab → New Query Group → New Source →*

   Excel Workbook → C:\Data\PowerBI-2\QMergeQuery.xlsx → `Open` *button → Select both Tables:*

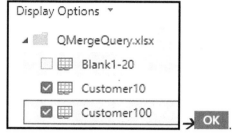

2. **Append:** *In Power Query Editor → Home Ribbon Tab → Combine Group → Append Queries dropdown → Append Queries As New*

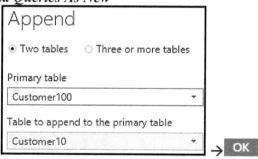

3. *Notice Record 101, Customer10 table was appended to Customer100 table.*
   Tip: This will create duplicate records.

99	99	99 Bordeaux Sports	Gerard
100	100	100 Arsenault et Maurier	Gaston
101	1	1 City Cyclists	Chris
102	2	2 Pathfinders	Christine
103	3	3 Bike-A-Holics Anonymous	Gary

Practice Exercise 58 - Append Two Tables

This will **Append** two separate **Tables** into a single **Table**. The **Relationships** will then need to be readjusted using a new combined **Table**. Make sure you have the **Customer** and **Orders** Tables open from the **BikeDB-B** data source.

1. **Begin a new blank Report:** *Start Power BI Desktop or start a new blank report (File Tab → New New).*

2. **Get Data:** *In Power BI → Home Ribbon Tab → Data Group → Get Data dropdown arrow →*

   Excel Workbook → C:\Data\PowerBI-2\QBikeDBCustOrder.xlsx → `Open` *button →*

   Select Sheet Customer and Orders → `Transform Data` *button.*

3. **New Source:** *In Power Query Editor → Home Ribbon Tab → New Query Group → New Source → Excel Workbook → C:\Data\PowerBI-2\QBikeDBAccessoryParts.xlsx Choose Accessary Table →*

4. **New Source:** *In Power Query Editor → Home Ribbon Tab → New Query Group → New Source → Excel Workbook → C:\Data\PowerBI-2\QBikeDBBicycleParts.xlsx Choose Bicycle Table →*

5. **Append:** *In Power Query Editor → Home Ribbon Tab → Combine Group → Append Queries dropdown → Append Queries As New → OK*.

6. *Review the Appended result*:

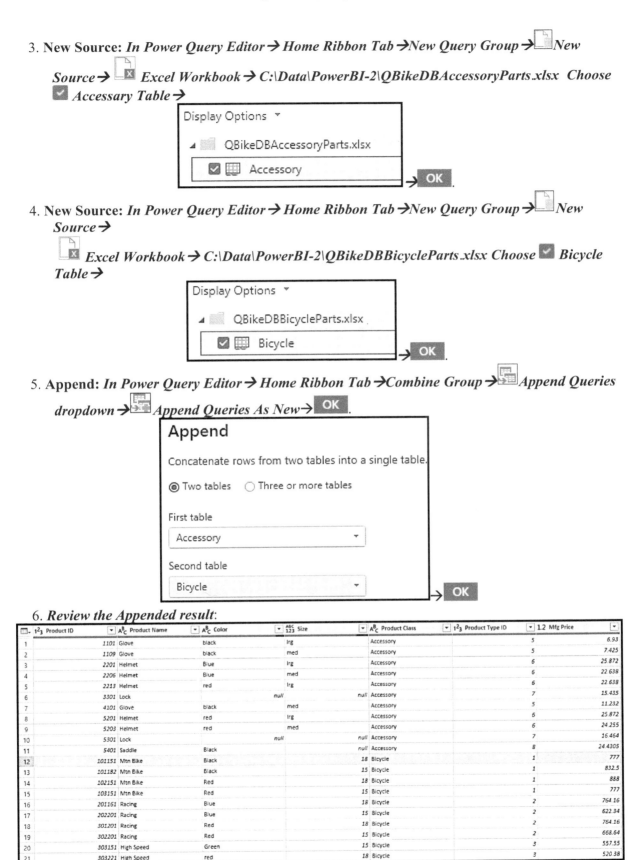

	1²₃ Product ID	Aᴮ꜀ Product Name	Aᴮ꜀ Color	ᴬᴮ꜀ Size	Aᴮ꜀ Product Class	1²₃ Product Type ID	1.2 Mfg Price
1	1101	Glove	black	lrg	Accessory	5	6.93
2	1109	Glove	black	med	Accessory	5	7.425
3	2201	Helmet	Blue	lrg	Accessory	6	25.872
4	2206	Helmet	Blue	med	Accessory	6	22.638
5	2213	Helmet	red	lrg	Accessory	6	22.638
6	3301	Lock	null	null	Accessory	7	15.435
7	4101	Glove	black	med	Accessory	5	11.232
8	5201	Helmet	red	lrg	Accessory	6	25.872
9	5203	Helmet	red	med	Accessory	6	24.255
10	5301	Lock	null	null	Accessory	7	16.464
11	5401	Saddle	Black	null	Accessory	8	24.4305
12	101151	Mtn Bike	Black	18	Bicycle	1	777
13	101182	Mtn Bike	Black	15	Bicycle	1	832.5
14	102151	Mtn Bike	Red	18	Bicycle	1	888
15	103151	Mtn Bike	Red	15	Bicycle	1	777
16	201161	Racing	Blue	18	Bicycle	2	764.16
17	202201	Racing	Blue	15	Bicycle	2	622.34
18	301201	Racing	Red	18	Bicycle	2	764.16
19	302201	Racing	Red	15	Bicycle	2	668.64
20	303151	High Speed	Green	15	Bicycle	3	557.55
21	303221	High Speed	red	18	Bicycle	3	520.38

7. **Rename Append1 Table to BicycleAccessory:** *In the Query Editor (left side of the interface) →Right-click on Append1 → Rename → BicycleAccessory.*

8. *Home Ribbon Tab →Close Group →Close and Apply.*

9. **Model View:** *In Power BI Interface choose Model View.*
   Remove unwanted Tables: *Right-click on the link →Press Delete.*
   Relink Orders: *Product ID to BicycleAccessory: Product ID by dragging and dropping the field name Product ID*

10. **The final relationships between Customer and Orders will look like the following:**

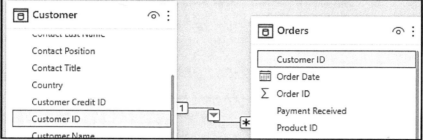

11. **The final relationships between Orders and BicycleAccessory will look like the following:**

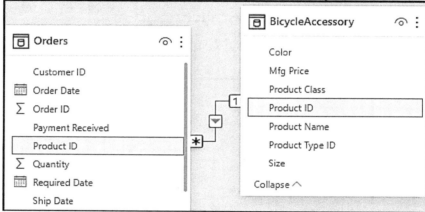

12. **Create a Stacked Column Chart:** *Select Staked Column Chart icon →Axis: BicycleAccessory Table →Product Name.* **Values:** *Orders Table →Total.*

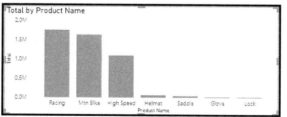 

2.34 Combine Files

Merge different columns from different files and place them into a single **Table**. For example, **Table1** could include product information and **Table2** could include order information. The **Combined Files** will create a single **Table** containing order information and product description added to the combined **Table**. All files must have a similar structure. Therefore, you will need to import all files into **Power BI** and possibly make changes to the **M Code**.

Practice Exercise 59 - Combine Files

1. **Create New Folder:** In **Windows,** create a new folder called **CombineFiles:**
   C:\Data\PowerBI-2\CombineFiles
2. **Copy Files:** In **Windows:** *Copy file "QAccounting1.xlsx" and "QAccounting2.xlsx" to folder*
   C:\Data\PowerBI-2\CombineFiles
3.  **Get Data Source:** *In Power BI→Home Ribbon Tab→Data Group→*  *Get Data dropdown arrow→More . . .→Folder→*

4. **Enter the folder path**: *Browse→*

5. **Inspect the Tables to be merged:**

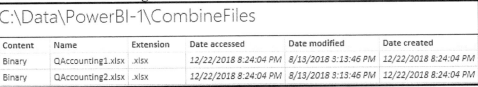

C:\Data\PowerBI-1\CombineFiles

Content	Name	Extension	Date accessed	Date modified	Date created
Binary	QAccounting1.xlsx	.xlsx	12/22/2018 8:24:04 PM	8/13/2018 3:13:46 PM	12/22/2018 8:24:04 PM
Binary	QAccounting2.xlsx	.xlsx	12/22/2018 8:24:04 PM	8/13/2018 3:13:46 PM	12/22/2018 8:24:04 PM

6. **Combine and Edit:** *Choose* **Combine & Transform Data** →

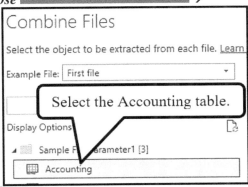

Select the Accounting table.

Complete: *Press* **OK** *to complete the Combine Query*.

7. The final result will combine both files and add a new field to identify a source file. Also, the **Combined Query** will be created in a new **Power BI Desktop**.

242	QAccounting1.xlsx	247	Offroad Bike Verleih	Large
243	QAccounting1.xlsx	248	Berg auf Trails GmBH.	Medium
244	QAccounting2.xlsx	1	City Cyclists	Large
245	QAccounting2.xlsx	2	Pathfinders	Medium
246	QAccounting2.xlsx	3	Bike-A-Holics Anonymous	Small Business
247	QAccounting2.xlsx	13	C-Gate Cycle Shoppe	Small Business

2.35 Text And Vision Analytics

This feature was added **Jun 2020 Update**.
Power Query →Home Ribbon Tab →AI Insights Group

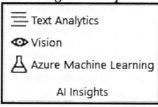

AI Insights

AI Insights for 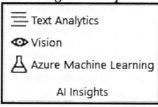 Text Analytics and Vision will allow you to access a collection of pre-trained machine learning models that will enhance your efforts to analyze information. The following services are supported:

Sentiment Analysis - This evaluates each line of text and returns a sentiment score ranging from zero (0) to one (1). It can be used in detecting positive or negative sentiment or tone in media reviews such as social media, book reviews, discussion forums, etc. The scores will fall between one (1) which indicates a positive score, and zero (0) which indicates a negative score.

Key Phrase Extraction - This will evaluate unstructured text and return a list of **Key Phrases**. These **Key Phrases** can be used to increase search keywords for web documentation.

Language Detection - This will detect and return the language name used. Currently, 120 languages are supported.

Image Tagging - This algorithm reviews images and recognizes objects in images such as living beings, actions indoor/outdoor settings, furniture, tools, plants, animals, accessories, gadgets, etc. It then issues a **Tag** for the type of object identified. **Tags** can then be further analyzed to determine the types of images found and categorize them. **Tip: Text** and **Vision Analysis** require **Power BI Premium**.

2.36 Azure Machine Learning

This feature was added in the **Jun 2020 Update**.

 Azure Machine Learning This feature will work with **Power BI Pro**, but you must have the proper **AI Data** stored in the **Azure Database**. It is also referred to as **Automated Machine Learning (AutoML) for Dataflows**. Building these models requires advanced training and a database containing the necessary data. However, this particular topic is beyond the capabilities of this current workbook.

Tip: The **Azure Machine Learning** model does not require **Power BI Premium,** only **Power BI Pro**.

Section 3 - Query Editor / Transform Ribbon Tab

The **Transform Ribbon Tab** changes or **Transforms** data such as **Adding** or **Removing Columns,** changing **Data Types, Splitting Columns,** or other data-driven tasks. The term **Transform Data** has to do with changing, filtering, adjusting, and shaping a **Data Table** to a new form or layout. The following is the **Transform Ribbon Tab.** All of these options will be covered in this section.

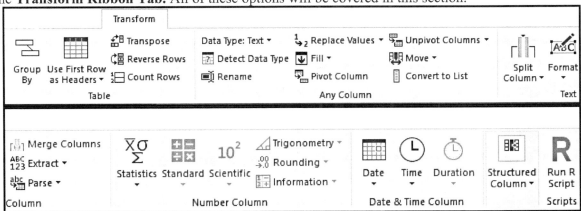

Section Table Of Contents

Practice Exercise 60 - Get Data QAccounting1

1. **New Report:** *Start Power BI Desktop or a new blank report (File Tab →* New *New).*

2. **Get Data Source:** *In Power BI Desktop →Home Ribbon Tab →Data Group → Get Data dropdown arrow → Excel Workbook → C:\Data\PowerBI-2\QAccounting1.xlsx →* Open *button.*

3. **Select Sheet:** *Choose the Accounting Sheet.*

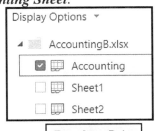

4. **Transform Data in the Query Editor:** Transform Data *button.* This will open the **Query Editor.**

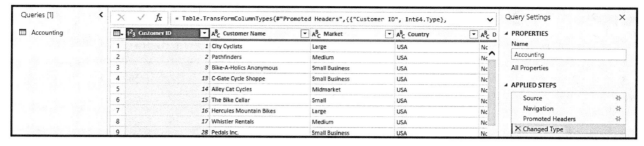

2.37 Group By

This will **Group** or summarize all related records in a column and apply a math operation either counting, summing, etc. It is also available in the **Home Ribbon Tab**. **Refer to Section 2 of this chapter**.

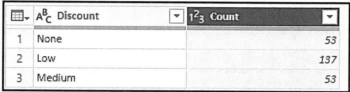

Practice Exercise 61 - Group By

1. **Select Table:** *Select the Accounting Table.*

2. **Duplicate Table:** *Home Ribbon Tab →Query Group → ⊞ Manage → 🗐 Duplicate.*

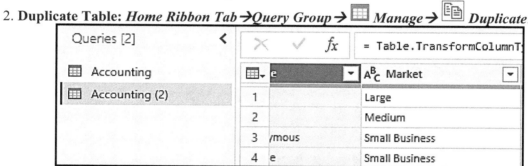

3. **Apply Group By to a new Table:** *Home Ribbon Tab →Transform Group →Group By.*

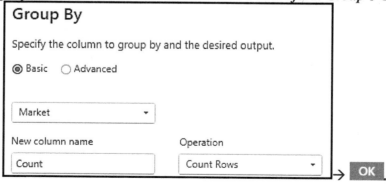

4. *View the Results:*

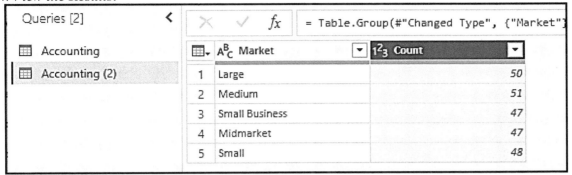

5. Remove the Applied Steps: *Click on the* ✕ *in the Applied Steps (located on the right side of the interface):* ✕ Grouped Rows

2.38 Use First Row As Headers

This will apply the **First Row** of a **Data Table** to the **Table** titles.

Tip: This command is available in the **Home Ribbon Tab**. <u>Refer to Section 2 of this chapter</u>.

Practice Exercise 62 - Use First Row As Header

Continue from the previous practice exercise.

1. *Select Accountng (2)→Transform Ribbon Tab→Table Group→Use First Row As Headers.*
Notice that the first row becomes the header:

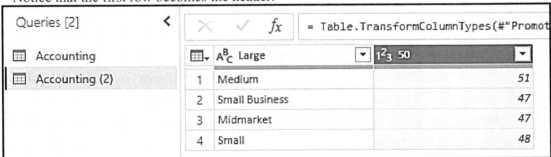

2. **Delete the Accounting (2) duplicate data source:** *Right-Click on Accounting (2)→* ✕ Delete .

Are you sure you want to delete 'Accounting (2)'? → Delete

2.39 Transpose

This switches all columns to rows, and rows to columns.

Practice Exercise 63 - Transpose

Continue from the previous practice exercise.

1. *Select* ⊞ Accounting *data source.*

2. **Enter Data:** *In Power Query Editor→Home Ribbon Tab→New Query Group→* ⊞ *Enter Data→ Enter values 1 through 20→ Name: Table1→* OK .

3. **Select Table:** Select **Query** called *Table1*.

4. **Transpose:** *Transform Ribbon Tab→Table Group→* [icon] *Transpose*.

5. **Reverse Transpose:** *Transpose Ribbon Tab→Table Group→* [icon] *Transpose*.

2.40 Reverse Rows

[icon] This will switch a **Table's Rows** (record). The first **Row** will be displayed on the last **Row** (record) and the last **Row** will be displayed on the top **Row**.

Practice Exercise 64 - Reverse Rows

Use *Table1* from the previous exercise.
1. **Select Table:** *Select Table1*.

2. **Reverse Rows:** *Transpose Ribbon Tab→ Table Group→* [icon] *Reverse Rows→ (review results)*.

3. **Return rows to the original setting:** *Transpose Ribbon Tab→ Table Group→* [icon] *Reverse Rows→(review results)*.

2.41 Count Rows

[icon] This will **Count** all the **Rows** and display a number of the total rows in a separate **Table**.

Practice Exercise 65 - Count Rows

1. **Select Table:** *In Power Query Editor→Select Accounting Table*.

2. **Duplicate Table:** *Right-click on Accounting Table→* [icon] *Duplicate→ Select the Duplicated Table*.

3. **Count Rows:** *Transpose Ribbon Tab → Table Group →* *Count Rows →(review results)*.

4. **Remove the Applied Steps:** *Press the* *in the following:* .

2.42 Data Type

This will change the **Data Type** of a column to a different type such as **Decimal Number, Whole Number, Date, Text**, etc. Refer to: *Home Ribbon Tab → Transform Group →Data Type* Chapter 2 Section 2 (for a detailed explanation).

2.43 Detect Data Type

This will review all records of a selected column to determine the **Data Type**. If it is still incorrect, use the **Data Type** command to force changes (if it was incorrectly imported) to the proper **Data Type**.
Select the desired column →Transform Ribbon Tab → Any Column Group →Detect Data Type.

2.44 Rename

One common use of the **Query Editor** is to **Rename** column labels into a more understandable name. These names will be used in **Reports** as the title.
Tip: You can **Rename** any column by double-clicking on a column label.

Practice Exercise 66 - Rename

1. **Select Table:** *In Power Query Editor →Select Accounting Table.*
2. **Rename:** *Select the* *column →Transform Ribbon Tab → Any Column Group →* *Rename →* .
3. **Remove the Applied Steps:** *Press the* *in the following:*
Tip: You can also double-click on a column label to rename a field.

2.45 Replace Values

This will find a specific value located in a **Data Table** and **Replace** every **Value** with a new one. Refer to the *Home Ribbon Tab → Transform Group →* *Replace Values* in:
Chapter 2 Section 2 of this Chapter.
Replace Errors - If a column has errors displayed, choose to **Replace Errors** with zero (0) or other text. *Transform Ribbon Tab → Any Column Group →* *Replace Values dropdown →* *Replace Errors.*

Practice Exercise 67 - Replace Values

1. **Select Table:** *In Power Query Editor→Select Accounting Table.*
2. **Replace Values:** *Select the Discount column* 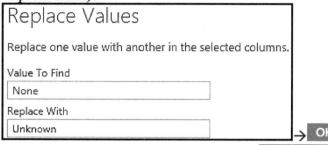 *→Transform Ribbon Tab→ Any Column Group→ Replace Values dropdown→ Replace Values → (enter the following and press* **OK** *):*

> Replace Values
>
> Replace one value with another in the selected columns.
>
> Value To Find
>
> None
>
> Replace With
>
> Unknown

→ **OK** .

3. **Remove the Applied Steps:** *Press the* ⊠ *in the following:* ✕ Replaced Value .

2.46 Fill

⬇ This **Fills** the values of cells that are blank with a record as shown in the value above.

Select the desired column→Transform Ribbon Tab→Any Column Group→ ⬇ Fill ▾ →
⬇ Down

In this example, the blank cells will be **Filled** with the value above them.

Before   After

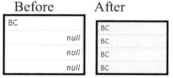

In this next example, the first is the origonal and the second is after the **Fill Down** was applied.

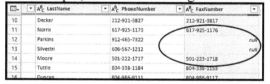 

2.47 Pivot Column

In the **Query Editor**, you can **Pivot** data in rows and columns. This will place a data record name as a new **Column** and all data associated with it will be placed under a **Column Name**. Select the desired **Column** and provide a numerical value to be used as a cross-section.

Practice Exercise 68 - Pivot Column

1. **Select Table:** *In Power Query Editor→Select Accounting Table.*
2. **Duplicate Column:** *Right-Click on the Accounting Table→* 📋*Duplicate.*
3. **Pivot Column:** *Select the Duplicated Table→ Select Discount*
A^B_C Discount ▾ *→Transform Ribbon Tab→ Any Column Group→* 🔲 *Pivot Column→*

This will list the **Discount Brand** fields in a column and compare all records to None, Low, Medium, and High. **Tip**: The **Pivot Column** will be moved to the far right side of the **Accounting Table**.

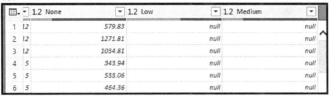

2.48 Unpivot Columns

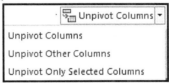 This removes a **Pivot** layout:

Unpivot Columns - This will **Unpivot** all **Columns**.
Unpivot Other Columns - This will **Unpivot Columns** not selected.
Unpivot Only Selected Columns - This will **Unpivot** selected **Columns**.

Practice Exercise 69 - Unpivot

Continue from the previous practice exercise.

1. **In the Query Editor:** *Home Ribbon Tab →New Query Group →* New Source → Excel Workbook →*C:\Data\PowerBI-2\QFilterPivotTable.xlsx →* Open button.
2. **Select Sheet:** *Choose the* PivotTable *Sheet →* OK.
   Tip: you should be in the **Query Editor and select the PivotTable data source**.
3. **Use First Row as Header:** *Select PivotTable Query →Transform Ribbon Tab → Table Group →* Use First Row as Headers ▾ *dropdown arrow →* Use First Row as Headers.
   Tip: You might need to do this twice until the **Header** has been restored.
4. **Select Columns:** *Administration, Development, Production, and Sales.*
5. **Unpivot Only Selected Columns:** *Unpivot Columns Dropdown →Unpivot Only Selected Columns.*

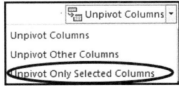

6. Notice the **Grand Total** is the same as the **Value Column**.
   The **Unpivot** command combined all selected **Columns** (Sales, Administration, Production, and

Development) to **Values**.

	A^B_C Row Labels		1^2_3 Grand Total		A^B_C Attribute		1^2_3 Value	
1	Abramas		57000		Sales			57000
2	Adelheim		33000		Administration			33000
3	Albrecht		51000		Production			51000
4	Bachman		55000		Development			55000
5	Baker		94000		Administration			29000

2.49 Move

This **Moves Columns** to a different position within a **Table**. **Tip:** This can also be done by selecting a **Column** and dragging it to another position. This will not change the original order in the **Table View**. But, the **Query Editor** will be reorganized to manage the **Columns** more effectively.

Practice Exercise 70 - Move

Select and **Move** the **Discount Column** to a new position.
1. **Select Table:** *In Power Query Editor→Select Accounting Table.*
2. **Move Right:** *Select the Discount Column→Transform Ribbon Tab→ Any Column Group→ Move dropdown→ Right.*
3. **Remove the Applied Steps:** *Press* ⊠ *in the following:* ⊠ Reordered Columns .

2.50 Convert To List

This **Converts** a selected **Column** to a single **Column List** of information. It removes all **Columns** except the final result of the **List**.
Tip: You might want to **Duplicate** the **Query** prior to using this command:

Home Ribbon Tab→ Query Group→ Manage dropdown→ Duplicate.

Practice Exercise 71 - Remove Duplicates From List

1. **Duplicate Table:** *In Power Query Editor→Select Accounting Table→Right-click on Accounting Table→ Manage→ Duplicate.*
2. **Convert to List:** *Select the Country column* A^B_C Country ▾ *→Transform Ribbon Tab→ Any Column Group→ Convert to List.*
    Tip: When the "**Convert To List**" is selected, there will be two **Transform Tabs**. Choose the one on on the right side of the ribbons.
3. **Remove Duplicates:** *Transform Contextual Ribbon Tab→ Remove Duplicates.*

Tip: There are two **Transform Ribbon Tabs**:

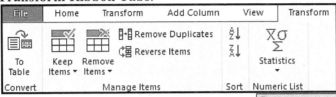

4. **Remove the Applied Steps:** *Press the* ☒ *in the following:* ✕ Removed Duplicates *and* ✕ Country

2.51 Split Columns

This will **Split** a single **Column** into two **Columns**.
Refer to *Home Ribbon Tab →Transform Group →Split Columns* in <u>Section 2 of this chapter.</u>

2.52 Format Button

 This will change all values in a selected **Column** to:

lowercase
UPPERCASE
Capitalize Each Word
Trim
Clean
Add Prefix
Add Suffix

Lowercase - This will convert all characters to **Lowercase**.
UPPERCASE - This will convert all characters to **Uppercase**.
Capitalize Each Word - This will convert all words in a **Column** to **Proper Case**.
Trim - This will **Trim** space characters before and after characters in a **Column**.
Clean - This will remove any non-printable characters contained in a **Column**.
Add Prefix - This will **Add** characters before data in a **Column**.
Add Suffix - This will **Add** characters to data in a column.

Tip: This feature is also available at *Add Column Ribbon Tab → From Text Group →* [A⁸C] *Format.*

Practice Exercise 72 - Uppercase

1. **Select Table:** *In Power Query Editor →Select Accounting Table.*

2. **Format Uppercase:** *Select column* A⁸C Discount ▼ *→Transform Ribbon Tab →*

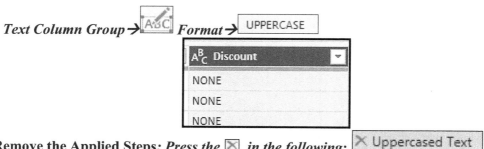

Text Column Group→ Format→ UPPERCASE

3. **Remove the Applied Steps**: *Press the* ⊠ *in the following:* ✕ Uppercased Text

2.53 Merge Columns

This will concatenate or patch several selected **Columns** into a **Single Column**. You must select the **Columns** to be Merged.

Tip: This feature is also available at: ***Add Column Ribbon Tab→From Text Group→*** Merge ***Columns*** located in: <u>**Section 2 of this chapter**</u>.

2.54 Extract

This will **Extract** specific characters from text values in a selected **Column**.
Tip: It might be valuable to keep the origonal **Column** and modify a duplicate **Column** using this command. See: ***Add Column Ribbon Tab→General Group→Duplicate Column***.

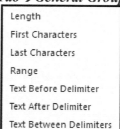

Length

First Characters

Last Characters

Range

Text Before Delimiter

Text After Delimiter

Text Between Delimiters

Tip: This feature is also available at: ***Add Column Ribbon Tab→ From Text Group→*** Extract.

Practice Exercise 73 - Extract

1. **Select Table**: ***In Power Query Editor→Select Accounting Table***.

2. **Extract First Character**: *Select the column* A^B_C Discount ***→Transform Ribbon Tab→Text Group→*** Extract***→First Characters***.

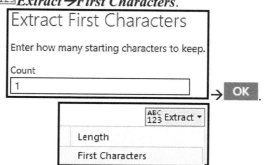

Extract First Characters

Enter how many starting characters to keep.

Count

1

→ **OK** .

ABC 123 Extract ▾

Length

First Characters

3. ***The end result will look similar to the following:***

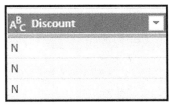

4. **Remove the Applied Steps:** *Press the* ⊠ *in the following:*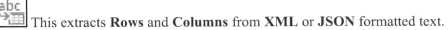

2.55 Parse

This extracts **Rows** and **Columns** from **XML** or **JSON** formatted text.

Tip: This feature is also available at *Add Column Ribbon Tab→Text Group→* Parse covered in <u>**Section 2 of this chapter.**</u>

2.56 Statistics

This will perform the following **Statistical** operations on a numeric **Column**:

The end result will provide a single total of the entire field. The following is the result:

Tip: This feature is also available at *Add Column Ribbon Tab → Add Number Group →* Statistics Covered in <u>**Section 2 of this chapter.**</u>

Practice Exercise 74 - Statistics

1. **Select Table:** *In Power Query Editor→Select Accounting Table.*

2. **Statistics Sum:** *Select the Units column* 1.2 Units →*Transform Ribbon Tab →Number Column Group →* Statistics →Sum.

396161

3. **Remove the Applied Steps:** *Press the* ⊠ *in the following:* ✕ Calculated Sum

2.57 Standard

This will perform the following **Standard** math functions on a numeric **Column**.

Tip: This feature is also available at *Add Column Ribbon Tab→ From Number Group→* Standard covered in <u>Section 2 of this chapter</u>.

> Add
> Multiply
> Subtract
> Divide
> Integer-Divide
> Modulo
> Percentage
> Percent Of

Practice Exercise 75 - Standard

This will add one (1) to every value in the field.

1. **Select Table:** *In Power Query Editor→Select Accounting Table.*
2. **Standard Add:** *Select* 1.2 GrossSales *column→Transform Ribbon Tab→Number Column Group→* Standard *dropdown→Add→(Enter the following value):*

> Add
>
> Enter a number to add to each value in the column.
>
> Value
>
> 1

→ OK

1.2 GrossSales
4141.62
8478.75
6898.71

Before:

1.2 GrossSales
4142.62
8479.75
6899.71

After:

3. **Remove the Applied Steps:** *Press the ⊠ in the following:*   ☓ Added to Column

2.58 Scientific

10² This will perform the following **Scientific** operations on a numeric **Column:**

> Absolute Value
> Power   ▶
> Square Root
> Exponent
> Logarithm   ▶

Power:

> Square
> Cube
> Power...

Logarithm:

> Base-10
> Natural

Tip: This feature is also available at: *Add Column Ribbon Tab→From Number Group→* 10² *Scientific.*

2.59 Trigonometry

◿ This will perform the following **Trigonometry** operations on a numeric **Column:**

Tip: This feature is also available at: *Add Column Ribbon Tab→From Number Group→* ◿ *Trigonometry* covered in <u>Section 2 of this chapter</u>.

Sine
Cosine
Tangent
Arcsine
Arccosine
Arctangent

2.60 Rounding

This **Rounds** decimal places using the following **Rounding** methods. **Tip:** This feature is also available at: ***Add Column Ribbon Tab→From Number Group→*** .00↴.0 ***Rounding*** covered in <u>Section 2 of this chapter</u>.

Round Up
Round Down
Round...

2.61 Information

This will create a **New Column** using the words **True** or **False** depending on the option chosen. Refer to ***Transform Ribbon Tab→ Number Column Group→*** ***Information*** covered in <u>Section 2 of this chapter</u>.

Practice Exercise 76 - Information

1. **Select Table:** *In Power Query Editor→Select Accounting Table*.

2. **Change Datatype:** *Select the MonthNum Column* 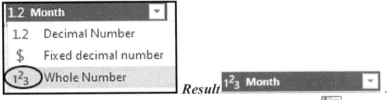 *→ Make sure the Data Type is a whole number*.

1.2 Month
  1.2 Decimal Number
  $ Fixed decimal number
  1²₃ Whole Number   *Result* 1²₃ Month .

3. **Set Is Even:** *Transform Ribbon Tab→ Number Column Group→* ***Information→Is Even***.

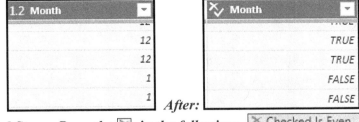

1.2 Month	X✓ Month
12	TRUE
12	TRUE
1	FALSE
1	FALSE

Before: *After:*

4. **Remove the Applied Steps:** *Press the* ☒ *in the following:* ☓ Checked Is Even

2.62 Date

This changes the look of a **Date t**o the following options. **Tip:** This feature is also available at: ***Add Column Ribbon Tab→ From Date & Time Group→*** ***Date*** covered in <u>Section 2 of this chapter</u>.

Practice Exercise 77 - Date

1. **Select Table:** *In Power Query Editor→Select Accounting Table*.
2. **Select Column:** *Select the Column*

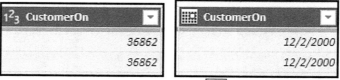

Tip: You may need to convert the field to the **Date** ▦ *Click the left side of the Field Name →* ▦*Date*.

3. **Set Date to Quarter:** *Transform Ribbon Tab → Date & Time Column Group →* ▦ *Date →Quarter → Quarter of Year*.

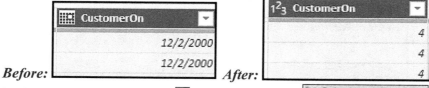

Before: **After:**

4. **Remove the Applied Steps:** *Press the* ☒ *in the following:* ✕ Calculated Quarter

2.63 Time

🕐 This will change the look of a **Time** value to the following options:

Tip: This feature is also available at: *Add Column Ribbon Tab → From Date & Time Group →* 🕐 *Time* covered in **Section 2 of this chapter**.

2.64 Duration

This will format a **Duration** field to the following types:
Tip: This feature is also available at: *Add Column Ribbon Tab → From Date & Time Group → Duration* covered in <u>Section 2 of this chapter</u>.

2.65 Run R Script

This performs transformation and shaping steps with **R Script Program Language**. You must have **R** installed in order to add **R Script**.

2.66 Python Script

This performs transformation and shaping steps with **Python Script Program Language**. You must have **Python** installed in order to add **Python Script**.

Section 4 - Query Editor / Add Column Ribbon Tab

The **Add Column** tab provides additional tasks associated with adding and manipulating **Columns**, formatting **Column** data, and adding custom **Columns**. The following is the **Add Column** tab:

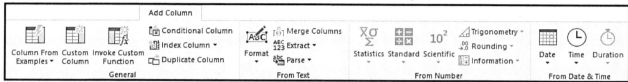

Section Table Of Contents

Practice Exercise 78 - Get Data QAccounting1

1. **New Blank Report:** *Start Power BI Desktop or a new blank report (File Tab →* New *New).*

2. **Get Data Source:** *In Power BI Desktop→Home Ribbon Tab→Data Group→* Get Data *dropdown arrow→* Excel Workbook → *C:\Data\PowerBI-2\QAccounting1.xlsx →* Open *button.*

3. **Select Sheet:** *Choose the Accounting Sheet.*

4. **Transform Data in the Query Editor:** Transform Data *button.* This will open the **Query Editor**.

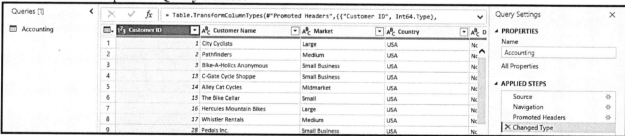

2.67 Column From Examples

This allows you to create a custom formula that will transform data into a **New Column**. The two options available are: **From All Columns** and **From Selection**.

From All Columns
From Selection

Practice Exercise 79 - Column From Examples

1. **Select Table:** *In Power Query Editor →Select Accounting Table.*

2. **Column From Examples:** *Add Column Ribbon Tab →General Group→ 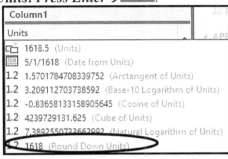 Column From Examples →From All Columns →(Type the words Units).*

3. **Choose Rounded Down Units:** *Press Enter→* `OK` .

Before: 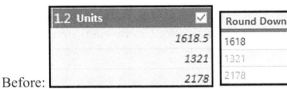 → `OK` → After: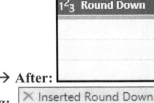

4. **Remove the Applied Steps:** *Press the* ☒ *in the following:* `✕ Inserted Round Down`

2.68 Custom Column

This will create a **New Column** using a formula from different fields.

The applied **Column** will appear in the **Applied Steps** (located on the right side of the interface). If you wish to remove the **Column** formula, you can delete the **Applied Step.**

Add Column Ribbon Tab →General Group→ Custom Column:

Practice Exercise 80 - Custom Column

Add a **Custom Column** to total the units sold at a sale price:

1. **Select Table:** *In Power Query Editor →Select Accounting Table.*

2. **Custom Column:** *Add Column Ribbon Tab →Custom Column →(use the Available columns on the right to spell the column names properly): Press* `OK` *and review the new field.*

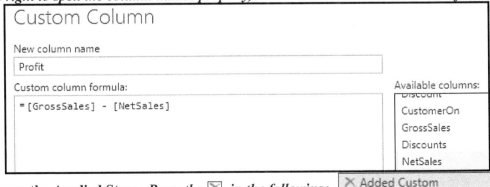

3. **Remove the Applied Steps:** *Press the* ☒ *in the following:* `✕ Added Custom` .

Test It: Add a **New Column** for the Year, Month, and Day.

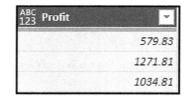

2.69 Invoke Custom Function

This will **Invoke** or execute a custom **Visual Basic** function such as:

Function TestFunc()
    MyVar = 2500
End Sub

In the **Invoke Custom Function** dialog box, insert the following: **MyFunc()**

2.70 Conditional Column

This will create a **New Column** from an existing **Column** using a **Conditional** statement.

Practice Exercise 81 - Conditional Column

1. **Select Table:** *In Power Query Editor→Select Accounting Table.*

2. **Conditional Column:** *Add Column Ribbon Tab →General Group →* ⊞ *Conditional Column →* *(Enter the following parameters)* **New Column Name**: *High GrossSales* **Operator**: *is greater than*

   Value: 🔲 *10000*

   Output: 🔲 *HighGS* (Tip: Change to [Select a column])

   Otherwise: 🔲 0 → **OK**.

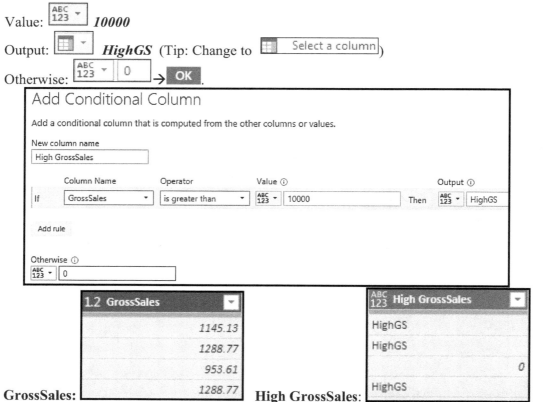

GrossSales: High GrossSales:

3. **Remove the Applied Steps:** *Press the* ☒ *in the following:* ☒ Added Conditional Column

2.71 Index Column

 This creates a **New Column** with a starting **Index**. The **Index** options are 0, 1, or a custom value. For example, using an Index of 0 will result in a **Column** numbered from 0,1,2,3, etc. This can be used if a **Table** does not have a key index field which can then be created.

Practice Exercise 82 - Index Column

Sort the **Segment Field** in ascending order and then create an **Index**.
1. **Select Table:** *In Power Query Editor→Select Accounting Table.*
2. **Select Field:** *Select Customer Name Field*

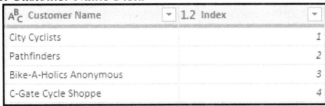

3. **Index Column:** *Add Column Ribbon Tab→General Group→ Index Column→From 1 →(review results)*

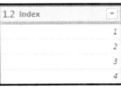

4. **Remove the Applied Steps:** *Press the ☒ in the following:* ☒ Added Index

2.72 Duplicate Column

This will make a copy of a selected **Column**.

Practice Exercise 83 - Duplicate Column

1. **Select Table:** *In Power Query Editor→Select Accounting Table.*

2. **Duplicate a Column:** *Select column Segment* [A^Bc Customer Name ▼] *→ Add Column Ribbon Tab→ Duplicate Column→(Review the Duplicated column).*

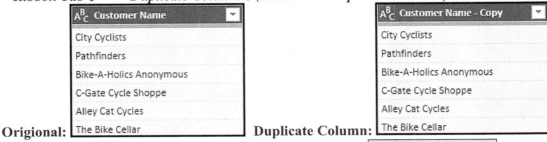

3. **Remove the Applied Steps:** *Press the ☒ in the following:* ☒ Duplicated Column .

2.73 Format Button

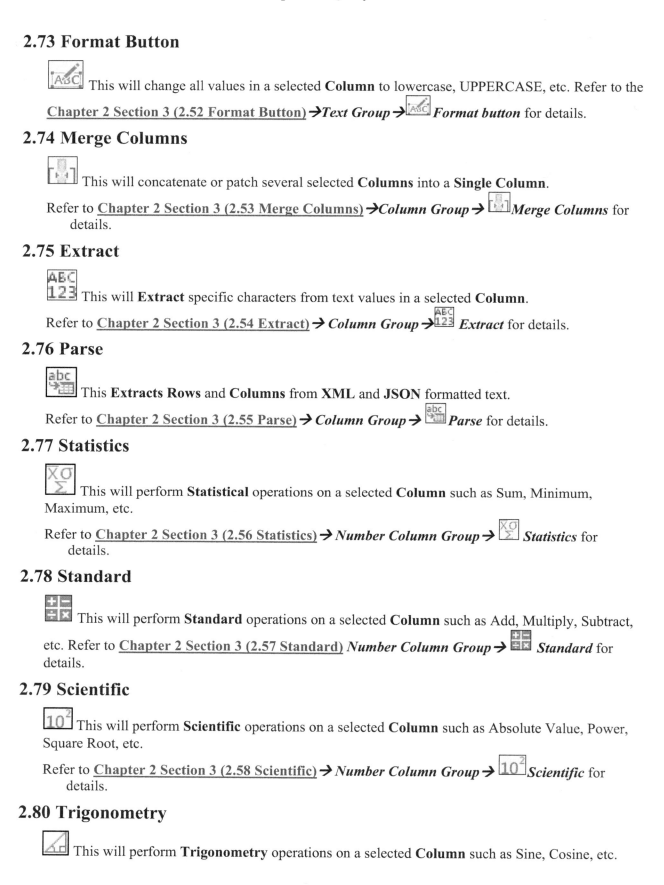 This will change all values in a selected **Column** to lowercase, UPPERCASE, etc. Refer to the

Chapter 2 Section 3 (2.52 Format Button) →*Text Group* → *Format button* for details.

2.74 Merge Columns

This will concatenate or patch several selected **Columns** into a **Single Column**.

Refer to Chapter 2 Section 3 (2.53 Merge Columns) →*Column Group* → *Merge Columns* for details.

2.75 Extract

This will **Extract** specific characters from text values in a selected **Column**.

Refer to Chapter 2 Section 3 (2.54 Extract) → *Column Group* → *Extract* for details.

2.76 Parse

This **Extracts Rows** and **Columns** from **XML** and **JSON** formatted text.

Refer to Chapter 2 Section 3 (2.55 Parse) → *Column Group* → *Parse* for details.

2.77 Statistics

This will perform **Statistical** operations on a selected **Column** such as Sum, Minimum, Maximum, etc.

Refer to Chapter 2 Section 3 (2.56 Statistics) → *Number Column Group* → *Statistics* for details.

2.78 Standard

This will perform **Standard** operations on a selected **Column** such as Add, Multiply, Subtract, etc. Refer to Chapter 2 Section 3 (2.57 Standard) *Number Column Group* → *Standard* for details.

2.79 Scientific

This will perform **Scientific** operations on a selected **Column** such as Absolute Value, Power, Square Root, etc.

Refer to Chapter 2 Section 3 (2.58 Scientific) → *Number Column Group* → *Scientific* for details.

2.80 Trigonometry

This will perform **Trigonometry** operations on a selected **Column** such as Sine, Cosine, etc.

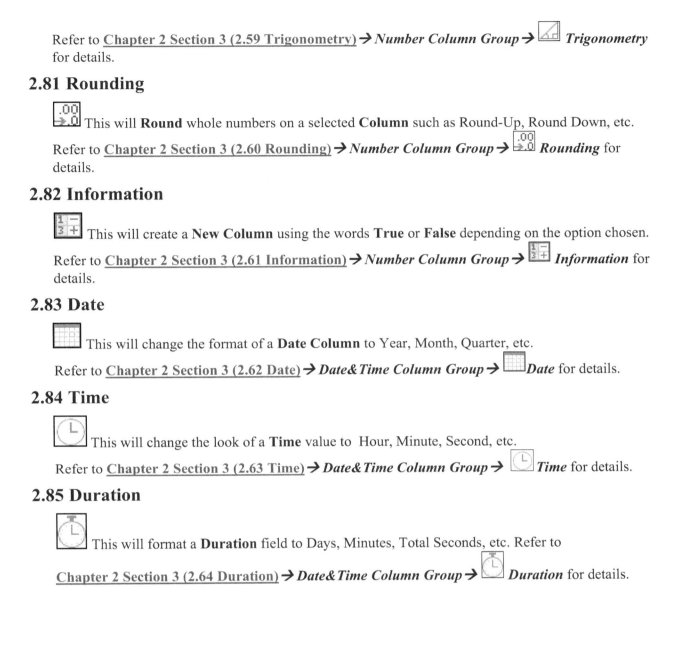

Refer to <u>Chapter 2 Section 3 (2.59 Trigonometry)</u> → *Number Column Group* → *Trigonometry* for details.

2.81 Rounding

This will **Round** whole numbers on a selected **Column** such as Round-Up, Round Down, etc.

Refer to <u>Chapter 2 Section 3 (2.60 Rounding)</u> → *Number Column Group* → *Rounding* for details.

2.82 Information

This will create a **New Column** using the words **True** or **False** depending on the option chosen.

Refer to <u>Chapter 2 Section 3 (2.61 Information)</u> → *Number Column Group* → *Information* for details.

2.83 Date

This will change the format of a **Date Column** to Year, Month, Quarter, etc.

Refer to <u>Chapter 2 Section 3 (2.62 Date)</u> → *Date&Time Column Group* → *Date* for details.

2.84 Time

This will change the look of a **Time** value to Hour, Minute, Second, etc.

Refer to <u>Chapter 2 Section 3 (2.63 Time)</u> → *Date&Time Column Group* → *Time* for details.

2.85 Duration

This will format a **Duration** field to Days, Minutes, Total Seconds, etc. Refer to

<u>Chapter 2 Section 3 (2.64 Duration)</u> → *Date&Time Column Group* → *Duration* for details.

Section 5 - Query Editor/View Ribbon Tab

The **View Ribbon Tab** on the **Query Editor** interface is used to toggle whether certain panes or windows are displayed. It is also used to display the **Advanced Editor**. The following image shows the **View Ribbon Tab:**

Section Table Of Contents

Practice Exercise 84 - Get Data BikeDB-B

1. **New Blank Report:** *Start Power BI Desktop or a new blank report (File Tab →* New *New).*

2. Get Data Source: *In Power BI Desktop →Home Ribbon Tab →Data Group → Get Data dropdown arrow → Excel Workbook →C:\Data\PowerBI-2\BikeDB-B.xlsx →* Open *button.*

3. **Select All Sheets:** *Select all 3 Sheets from Excel →* Transform Data *button.* (This will open the **Query Editor**).

4. **In Power Query Editor:** *View Ribbon Tab →Dependencies Group →* Query Dependencies

2.86 Query Settings

The **Query Settings** are displayed on the right side of the interface and contain two major options: *Select the Products Table →In Power Query Editor →View Ribbon Tab →Layout Group →* Query Settings:

1. **Properties -** The most important purpose of **Properties** is to rename a **Query**.
2. **Applied Steps -** Whenever you add a **Query** step or the filter in the **Query Editor,** it is inserted into the sequence of steps located in the **Query Settings/Applied Steps**. Usually, steps are added at the end of a sequence. However, if you add a step anywhere other than at the end of the flow, you should verify that all subsequent steps function properly. The screen above is an example of the **Applied Steps** located on the right side of the interface.

2.87 Formula Bar

☑ This will display the **Formula Bar** similar to the **Excel Formula Bar**. It will allow you to see the code that is being used to build each step in the **Query Settings/Applied Steps**. The equation is using **M Language** to transform data, and the dropdown arrow located on the right side of the **Formula Bar** is used to expand it in order to view more code.

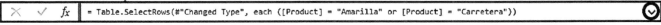

```
× ✓ fx   = Table.SelectRows(#"Changed Type", each ([Product] = "Amarilla" or [Product] = "Carretera"))
```

2.88 Monospaced

☑ This displays data using a **Monospaced Font** which is a lighter gray shade.
The following will show the differences:
☐ **Monospace Unchecked**:

1²₃ Product ID	AᴮC Product Name	AᴮC Color
1	1101 Glove	black
2	1109 Glove	black
3	2201 Helmet	Blue

☑ **Monospace Checked:**

1²₃ Product ID	AᴮC Product Name	AᴮC Color
1	1101 Glove	black
2	1109 Glove	black
3	2201 Helmet	Blue

2.89 Show Whitespace

☑ This displays white space in the background. In some versions, this has no apparent effect.

1²₃ Product ID	AᴮC Product Name	AᴮC Color
1	1101 Glove	black
2	1109 Glove	black
3	2201 Helmet	Blue

2.90 Column Quality

☑ **Column Quality:**
If you display **100%**, then the **Column** does not contain **Blank/Empty** records. The **Column Quality** will display the status.

1²₃ Product ID		AᴮC Product Name		AᴮC Color	
● Valid	100%	● Valid	100%	● Valid	90%
● Error	0%	● Error	0%	● Error	0%
● Empty	0%	● Empty	0%	● Empty	10%
1	1101	Glove		black	
2	1109	Glove		black	

2.91 Column Distribution

☑ **Column Distribution:**

This tells you the number of records that are **Distinct** or **Unique** records in a **Column**.

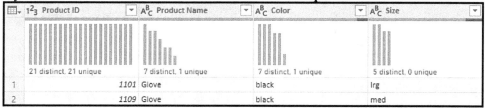

2.92 Column Profile

☑ **Column Profile:**

This provides a status of the data in a **Column**.

	1²₃ Product ID	A^B_C Product Name	A^B_C Color	A^B_C Size	A^B_C Product Class	1²₃ Product Type ID
1	1101	Glove	black	lrg	Accessory	
2	1109	Glove	black	med	Accessory	
3	2201	Helmet	Blue	lrg	Accessory	
4	2206	Helmet	Blue	med	Accessory	
5	2213	Helmet	red	lrg	Accessory	
6	3301	Lock	null	null	Accessory	
7	4101	Glove	black	med	Accessory	
8						

Column statistics ...

Count	21
Error	0
Empty	0
Distinct	7
Unique	1
Empty string	0
Min	Glove
Max	Saddle

Value distribution ...

Helmet
Mtn Bike
Racing
Glove
Lock
High Speed
Saddle

2.93 Go To Column

This will find a **Column** located in large **Tables**. Refer to:

Home Ribbon Tab→Manage Columns Group→ *Choose Column* for a detailed explanation.

2.94 Always Allow

☑ **Checking** this will **Always Allow** parameterization in a data source and transformation dialogs. It is not ☐ **Checked** by default. Therefore, if you encounter problems with parameters and prompts, this may correct the problem.

2.95 Advanced Editor

The **Advanced Editor** is where filtering steps are associated with a **Table** using the **Query Formula Language**. It is often referred to as the **M Program Language**.

Refer to ***Home Ribbon Tab→Query Group→*** *Advanced Editor* for a detailed explanation.
Tip: This can also be accessed by: ***In Power BI→Home Ribbon Tab→Queries***

Group →▦ Transform Data →Right-Click on any Table located on the left side of the interface →Advanced Editor.

2.96 Query Dependencies

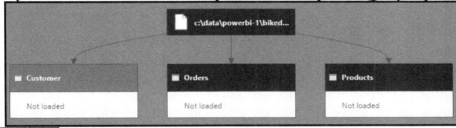
The **Query Dependencies** button displays how multiple **Tables** are related together. Often, this is done automatically. The **Query Dependencies** button will display the following dialog box: ***In Power Query Editor →View Ribbon Tab →Dependencies Group → Query Dependencies.***

Layout — The following layouts are available:

✓	Top to Bottom Layout
	Bottom to Top Layout
	Left to Right Layout
	Right to Left Layout

Zoom In/Out — This will scale the **Query Dependencies** larger/smaller.

Fit To Screen — When you scale in, a **Query** may disappear off the viewable dialog box. Therefore, this tool will fit everything into the viewable area.

Reduce Viewable Screen - If you hold the cursor on the bottom of the dialog box, a line with arrows on each side will appear. This will allow you to reduce the viewable area.

Practice Exercise 85 - Query Dependencies

1. **Query Dependencies:** *In Power Query Editor →View Ribbon Tab → Dependencies Group → Query Dependencies.*

2. **Test It:** Use the following to adjust the diagram: *Reduce Viewable Area, Fit to Screen, Zoom In/Out, and the different layouts.*

Chapter 3 - DAX Formula Overview

This chapter will provide an overview of the most important **DAX** formulas, functions, and capabilities. First, we will review the common settings to better create formulas; then, we will review ⊞ **New Column**, 🔢 **New Measure**, ⊡ **New Table**, and 🔢 **Quick Measure**.

Chapter Table Of Contents

Section 1 - DAX Overview

We will first discuss the basic **DAX** structure and define the development techniques.

Section Table Of Contents

Practice Exercise 86 - Open AccountingA

1. In **Power BI Desktop:** *File Tab→Open→ C:\Data\PowerBI-2\AccountingA.pbix→* [Open] **Button.** This will open a **Power BI** file containing the following **Visual Reports:**

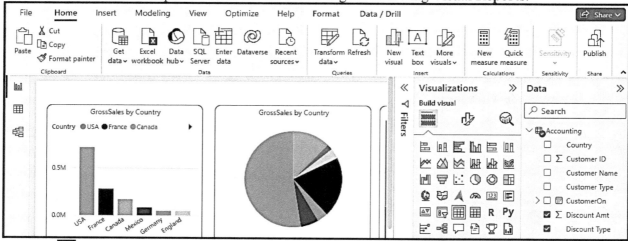

2. In ⊞ *Table View button (located on the left side of the screen)*

3.1 Functions

Functions are predefined formulas such as Sum, Average, or Count. There are many different types of **Functions** such as Date, Time, Information, Logical, Mathematical, Statistical, Text, and Time Intelligence **Functions**. If you are familiar with **Excel** functions, **DAX** provides a similar capability. However, **DAX Functions** are unique in the following ways:

1. A **DAX Function** always references a complete column or a table.

2. Some **DAX Functions** have built-in filters.

3. **DAX Functions** can be applied to a ⊞ **New Column**, ⊞ **New Measure**, and ⊞ **New Table**. (See below for a complete understanding).

3.2 Row Context

Row Context is most easily thought of as data or a record located in the current row. For example, when Quantity * Price is multiplied, it will calculate the total cost of each row of a table. If a column has a filter applied, you will only see calculations for the filtered result. **Row Context** is usually applied to **Measures.**

Unit Price ▼	Quantity ▼
1592	3
1592	3
1592	3

3.3 Filter Context

This is a unique **DAX** feature because it differs from **Excel** functions. It is built into several **DAX** functions to reduce or **Filter** the records being processed. For example, if you are processing a formula on a row-by-row basis, you can apply a **Filter** after the result of each row calculation. Some common **Filter Context** functions include **All, Related, Filter,** and **Calculate.** This can be applied to a ⊞ **New Column**, ⊞ **New Measures,** and ⊞ **New Table** which are different methods used to create formulas in **Power BI.**

Practice Exercise 87 - Filter Context

The 2nd part of the calculate function is the **Filter Context.**
Modeling Ribbon Tab →Calculations Group →New Measure →
Total = Calculate(Sum([GrossSales]), Accounting[Customer Type]="Small") → ☑ Commit.

```
✕ ✓ | 1 Total = Calculate(Sum([GrossSales]), Accounting[Customer Type]="Small")
```

3.4 Formula Editor

In the **Dec 2019 Update,** the code in the formula bar can be expanded to the entire screen and you can zoom in using the [Ctrl] [+] / [-] keys or **Roller** on the **Mouse.**

Practice Exercise 88 - Formula Editor

Modeling Ribbon Tab →Calculations Group →New Measure →Press* [Ctrl] [+] *key→* [Ctrl] [-] *key→

Press the [∨] ***dropdown arrow (located on the right side of the formula bar).***

```
✕ ✓ | 1 Measure =                                                          ∨
```

3.5 Cancel Formula

✕ When you are creating a formula in the formula bar, the leftmost button is the ✕ **Cancel** button. If you create a **New Measure** or **Column,** then, press the X to cancel. It will abort whatever was typed in.

Practice Exercise 89 - Cancel Formula

Modeling Ribbon Tab → Calculations Group → ⊞ ***New Column→*** ✕ .

```
✕ ✓ | Measure =
```

3.6 Commit Formula

The **Checkmark** button will **Check** the **Formula** syntax for correctness, and it isn't active until you enter in a formula. If you create a **New Measure** or **Column**, press the to **Check** the formula for syntax errors. *Modeling Ribbon Tab → New Column → Commit.*

Practice Exercise 90 - Commit Formula

Modeling Ribbon Tab → Calculations Group → New Column → Type in the following:
Measure1 = Sum(Accounting[GrossSales]) → Commit.

```
X  ✓  1 Measure1 = Sum(Accounting[GrossSales])          ⌄
```

3.7 IntelliSense

In the formula bar, type the formula name, then type an equal sign =. To add a field, press the open bracket [. You'll see that a small window appears with all of the field names listed. After typing the opening parenthesis for a formula, the **IntelliSense** capability shows you the parameters required for the specified function. The [will display the fields available and then, typing a letter that begins with a function name will display the available functions.

Practice Exercise 91 - IntelliSense

Modeling Ribbon Tab → Calculations Group → New Column → Type: Column = [

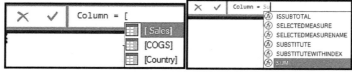

3.8 Data Types

When you **Import** or **Get Data** into a **Power BI**, the data is converted to one of the following **Data Types**.

Decimal Number
Fixed decimal number
Whole Number
Date/Time
Date
Time
Text
True/False
Binary

Whole Numbers - These are integers that have no decimal places. They can be positive or negative numbers in the range from -9,223,372,036,854,775,808 (-2^{63}) and 9,223,372,036,854,775,807 ($2^{63}-1$).

Decimal Numbers - These are real numbers that can have decimal places. Real numbers cover a wide range of values: Negative values from -1.79E +308 through 2.23E -308, Zero or Positive values from 2.23E -308 through 1.79E + 308.

TRUE/FALSE - This is a **Boolean** value that is either **True** or **False**.

Text - This is a character data string containing strings, numbers, or dates represented in a text format. Maximum string length is 268,435,456 Unicode characters (256 mega characters) or 536,870,912 bytes.

Date/time - This will accept most **Date/Time** representations when entered. Valid dates are all dates after January 1, 1900.

Currency - This **Data Type** allows values between -922,337,203,685,477.5808 to 922,337,203,685,477.5807 with four decimal digits of fixed precision.

N/A or Blank - A **Blank** is a **Data Type** in **DAX** that represents and replaces **SQL** nulls. You can create a **Blank** by using the **BLANK** function, and you can test for **Blanks** by using the logical function, **ISBLANK**.

Practice Exercise 92 - Column Tools Data Type

Select ☐ ∑ NetSales ··· *(in the field List) →Column Tools Ribbon Tab →Format: Currency.*

$% Format Currency ⌄

3.9 Arithmetic Operators

These are the basic mathematical operations:

+ (plus sign) - This will add two values. Example: *3+3*

- (minus sign) - This will subtract two numbers or indicate negative numbers. Example: *3-1-1*

* (asterisk) - This will multiply two numbers. Example: *3*3*

/ (forward slash) - This will divide two numbers, Example: *3/3*

^ (caret) - This will calculate an Exponent. Example: *16^4*

3.10 Calculation Order

Expressions are always read from left to right, but multiplication and division will be processed before plus/minus operators. To change the order of processing, place the parentheses around the formula and that specific part will be calculated first. The following are a few examples:

= 5 + 2 * 3 - This will always perform multiplication/division before addition/subtraction similar to **Excel**.

= (5 + 2) * 3 - This will calculate the values in the parentheses first.

=5 / 3 * 2 - When you must divide and multiply in the same statement, you perform the operation in visual order. Some make the mistake of always multiplying first then dividing.

= (3 + 0.25) / (3 - 0.25) - This will calculate the values in parentheses first.

= -2^2 - The exponentiation operator is applied before multiplication/division and the result is -4.

= (-2)^2 - The exponentiation operator is applied first and the result is 4.

Practice Exercise 93 - Order Of Arithmetic Operators

Modeling Ribbon Tab →Calculations Group →New Measure →Order = 5+2*3 → ☑ Commit.

X ✓ 1 Order: 5+2*3

Practice Exercise 94 - Calculation Order

First do the following equation manually using a calculator *3(5 + 20 / 2 x 5)*

Modeling Ribbon Tab →Calculations Group →New Measure →Enter the following:

Order2 = 3 * (5 + 20 / 2 * 5) → ☑ Commit.

X ✓ 1 Order2 = 3 * (5 + 20 / 2 * 5)

📊 *Report View →*🔢 *Card Icon →Place the Order 2 field in the card.*

165.00
Order2

Tip: The manual order of calculation is:
1) 3(5 + 20 / 2 * 5) - The division is performed first: 20 /2.
2) 3(5 + 10 X 5) - The multiplication is next: 10 x 5.
3) 3(5 + 50)   - Complete the values in the parentheses: 5 + 50.
4) 3(55)   - Then, multiply 3 x 55.
5) 165 - Answer. If you did the multiplication in step2 first, you would get a wrong answer.

3.11 Nesting

DAX formulas can contain up to 64 **Nested** functions. However, it is unlikely a formula would ever contain so many **Nested** functions. Such a formula would be very difficult to create and debug. Also, it would probably be executed very slowly.

Practice Exercise 95 - Nest Formula

> *Modeling Ribbon Tab →Calculations Group →New Measure →Enter the following:*
>
> *Measure 3 = Sum(Accounting[GrossSales]) →Add to formula:*
>
> *Measure 3=CALCULATE(Sum(Accounting[GrossSales]),Accounting[Customer Type]="Large")*

```
X ✓  1 Measure 3 = CALCULATE(Sum(Accounting[GrossSales]), Accounting[Customer Type]="Large")
```

3.12 Comments

Comments can be inserted in a formula to clarify or provide information for the code. In order to insert a **Comment,** place a // character at the beginning of the line in front of the text and press Shift Enter keys or Alt Enter keys.

Example: // This is a comment.

Practice Exercise 96 - Comment

> 1. *Modeling Ribbon Tab →Calculations Group →New Measure →Enter the following:*
>
> Total = Calculate(Sum([GrossSales]), Accounting[Customer Type]="Small") → ☑.
>
> 2. *Press Shift Enter keys →Type in the following:*
>
> // The above formula will filter and display only the Small Customer Type→ ☑.
>
> 3. The result:

```
X ✓  1 Total = Calculate(Sum([GrossSales]), Accounting[Customer Type]="Small")
     2 // The above formula will filter and display only the Small Customer Type
```

3.13 Comparison Operators

You can **Compare** two values with the following **Operators**. When two values are **Compared** by using these **Operators**, the result is a logical value, and the answer is either TRUE or FALSE.

= - This is an **Equal to** symbol. Example: *[Region] = "USA"*

\> - This is a **Greater Than** symbol. Example = *[Sales Date] > "Jan 2009"*

< - This is a **Less Than** symbol. Example = *[Sales Date] < "Jan 1 2009"*

\>= - This is a **Greater Than or Equal To** symbol. Example = *[Amount] >=20000*

<= - This is a **Less Than or Equal To** symbol. Example = *[Amount] <= 100*

<> - This is a **Not Equal To** symbol. Example = *[Region] <> "USA"*

Practice Exercise 97 - Comparison Operators

Modeling Ribbon Tab→ Calculations Group→ 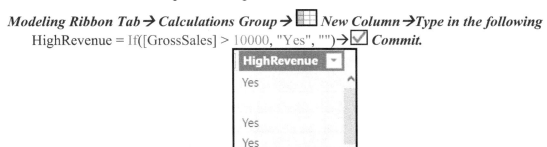 *New Column→Type in the following*
HighRevenue = If([GrossSales] > 10000, "Yes", "")→☑ *Commit.*

3.14 Move Formula

This will **Move** a **Formula** to a different location in the **Field List**. When you create a **New Measure**, you need to select a field in the proper table located in the **Field List** on the right side of the screen. If you create the **New Measure** in the wrong table, this feature will move it to the proper table. For example, if you create a **Measure** using fields in the **Orders** table, you need to select any field in the **Orders** table when you begin the Measure.

Practice Exercise 98 - Move Measure

To move a Measure to the orders table:
1. **Create a Measure:** *Select the Accounting table in the field list.*

2. **Create a new table:** *Modeling Ribbon Tab→* New Table→Enter the following:
    Table = All(Accounting, [GrossSales]) →☑ Commit.
    ```
    X ✓  -1 Table = All(Accounting[GrossSales])
    ```

3. Create a Measure: *Select the Accounting table (in the field list) →Modeling Ribbon Tab→*
    New Measure→ MyMeasure = Sum(Accounting, [GrossSales]) →☑ Commit.
    ```
    X ✓  -1 MyMeasure = Sum(Accounting[GrossSales])
    ```

4. *Select MyMeasure (located in the Accounting Table) → Measure Tools Contextual Ribbon Tab →Home Table: Table.*

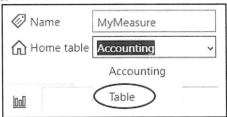

Section 2 - New Column

This will create a **New Column** using a **DAX** statement.

Section Table Of Contents

Practice Exercise 99 - Open BikeDB-B

1. In **Power BI Desktop**: *File Tab→Open →C:\Data\PowerBI-2\AccountingB.pbix→* Open **Button.** This will open a **Power BI** file containing the following **Visual Reports**:

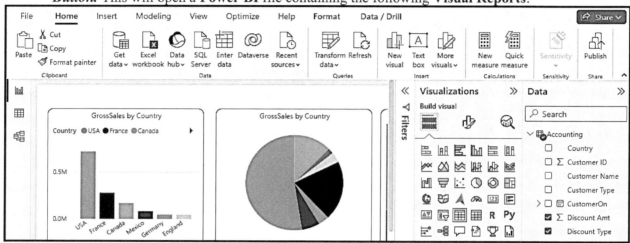

3.15 New Column

This will allow you to add a new field to an existing table. The **Column** that is created can be a combination of other **Columns** or can contain a mathematical calculation. **Calculated Columns** will appear in the **Fields** list just like any other field, but they'll have a special icon showing that their values are the result of a formula. You can name your **Columns** whatever you want and add them to a report visualization just like other fields.

```
X  ✓  1 Column =
```

Practice Exercise 100 - Math Manipulation Column

This will calculate a math operation on each row and place the result in a **New Column**.

1. *Modeling Ribbon Tab→ New Column→Enter the following:*

Amt Per Unit = [GrossSales]/[Units]→ ✓ *Commit.* The following is the code in the **Formula Bar**:

```
X  ✓  1 Amt Per Unit = [GrossSales]/[Units]
```

2. In **Table View**: *Table View→Review the* Amt Per Unit *column.*
3. Review the ☑ 📊 Amt Per Unit located in the field list.

Tip: Add a **Round Function** to reduce decimal places. Example:

Amt Per Unit = Round([GrossSales]/[Units], 2)

3.16 Concatenation Operator

Use the **Ampersand (&)** to **Join**, or **Concatenate** two or more text strings to produce a single piece of text. Example = *[Region] & ", " & [City]*

Practice Exercise 101 - Percentage Column

Calculate the **Sales Percentage by Country**.

1. *Modeling Ribbon Tab→* ▦ *New Column →Enter the following:*
   Sales Discount % = Round(([Discount Amt]/[GrossSales])*100, 0) & "%" → ☑ *Commit.*
   The following is the code in the **Formula Bar**:

2. In **Table View**: ▦ *Table View→Review the* [Sales Discount % ▼] *column.*
3. Review the ☐ 📊 Sales Discount % located in the field list.
   Tip: The result will be a text string, not a percentage numeric value, but it will visibly display as a percentage value.

Practice Exercise 102 - Concatenation

This will concatenate or patch two columns into a single new column.

1. *Modeling Ribbon Tab→* ▦ *New Column →Enter the following:*
   Name Type = [Customer Name] & "-" & [Customer Type] → ☑ *Commit.*
   The following is the code in the **Formula Bar**:

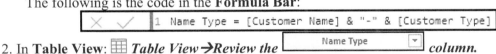

2. In **Table View**: ▦ *Table View→Review the* [Name Type ▼] *column.*
3. Review the new Field.

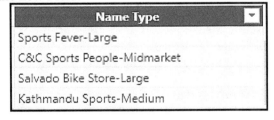

Section 3 - New Measures

Measures are a **DAX** formula created to analyze data using functions such as **Sums, Averages, Minimum** or **Maximum** values, **Counts**, static values, or more advanced calculations. These **DAX** formulas can be used as input into other **DAX** formulas, and in **Power BI Desktop**, **Measures** are created and used in the **Report** or ⊞ **Table View**. After you finalize a **Measure,** they will appear in the **Fields** list with a calculator icon.

Section Table Of Contents

Practice Exercise 103 - Open AccountingA

1. In **Power BI Desktop**: *File Tab→Open→C:\Data\PowerBI-2\AccountingA.pbix→* Open **Button.**
This will open a **Power BI** file containing the following **Visual Reports**:

3.17 Measure

You can name **Measures** whatever you want and add them to a new or existing **Visualization** just like any other field. Often, an aggregate formula (**Sum, Average**, etc.) is placed in a **Card** or **Table Report**. The following are two different types of measures:

Implicit Measures - This is a technique used to place fields in the **Values** drop-box in an **Excel Pivot Table** without building a formula to calculate it. The result doesn't sum up a single field but calculates the cross-section between the column and row. The **Implicit Measure** is not a formula, but a field used as a formula.

Explicit Measures - These are actual **DAX** formulas that use existing fields to calculate a new result. **Explicit Measures** are necessary when using the **Analyze In Excel** command in **Power BI Pro Web**. Without an **Explicit Measure,** you will not be able to **Analyze** data in **Excel.** View the next few **practice exercises** and the next **student project** to better understand **Implicit** and **Explicit Measures.**

Practice Exercise 104 - Sum of Gross Sales

Create a **Measure** to calculate the total **Gross Sales**.

1. *Modeling Ribbon Tab→* 🖩 *New Measure→Enter the following:*
   Total Gross = Sum([GrossSales]) → ☑ *Commit.*
   The following is the code in the **Formula Bar**

   ```
   1  Total Gross = Sum([GrossSales])
   ```

2. Create **Card Report:** 📊 *Report View→* 🔢 *Card→Drag* ☑ 🖩 Total Gross *field to the Card.*

   Card Result:

   > 1.36M
   > **Total Gross**

Practice Exercise 105 - Filtered GrossSales

Calculate Gross Sales for the Small Customer Type.

1. *Modeling Ribbon Tab→* 🖩 *New Measure→Enter the following:*
   Adj Total Gross=Calculate(Sum([GrossSales]), Accounting[Customer Type]="Small") → ☑
   Commit.
   The following is the code in the **Formula Bar**:

   ```
   1  Adj Total Gross=Calculate(Sum([GrossSales]), Accounting[Customer Type]="Small")
   ```

2. Create **Card Report:** 📊 *Report View→* 🔢 *Card→Drag* ☑ 🖩 Adj Total Gross *field to the*
   Card.
   Tip: The first parameter of the **Calculate** function is to **Sum** the **GrossSales** field and the second
   parameter is the **Filter**.

   Card Result:

   > 277.99K
   > **Adj Total Gross**

Practice Exercise 106 - Last Refresh

This will display the last time the report was refreshed.

1. *Get Data→Blank Query→Enter the following: DateTime.LocalNow()* → ☑.

   ```
   fx   = DateTime.LocalNow()
   ```

2. **Rename the new query to:** *LastRefresh*

   Queries

   ▦ Accounting
   ᴬᴮ𝒸 LastRefresh *→Home Ribbon Tab→* 🗙 *Close & Apply.*

3. *Create a Card:* 🔢 *Card icon→ In the field list, Place the Last Refresh field in the Card.*

   > 11/27/2023 4:12:05 PM
   > Earliest LastRefresh

Section 4 - New Table

Tables can be created from existing **Tables** in the **Power Query Editor** or from a **DAX** formula in the **Table View**. In this section, we will create **Tables** using the **DAX Program Language**.

Section 4 - New Table

Practice Exercise 107 - Open AccountingA

1. In **Power BI Desktop**: *File Tab→Open→C:\Data\PowerBI-2\AccountingA.pbix→* Open Button.
This will open a **Power BI** file containing the following **Visual Reports**:

3.18 New Table

This will create a New Table by applying a **DAX** formula and filters. You can take full advantage of the **Filter Context** discussed in the next chapter. The New Table is based on existing tables and can maintain established relationships.

Practice Exercise 108 - Create Duplicate Table

Create a duplicate of the **Accounting** table.

1. *Modeling Ribbon Tab→ New Table→Enter the following: Table1 = Accounting*
The following is the code in the **Formula Bar**:

```
1 Table1 = Accounting
```

2. Select and review Table 1 located in the field list under the Accounting table.

Practice Exercise 109 - Create Table of Country Field

Create a **New Table** containing only the **Country** field.

1. *Modeling Ribbon Tab→ New Table→Enter the following:*
Table2 = All(Accounting[country]) The following is the code in the **Formula Bar**:

```
1 Table2 = All(Accounting[country])
```

2. Select and review Table 2 located in the field list under the Accounting table.

Practice Exercise 110 - Create Table Using The AllExcept Filter

Create a duplicate of the **Accounting** table and remove the **Country** field.

1. ***Modeling Ribbon Tab→*** 🔲 ***New Table→Enter the following:***
   Table3 = AllExcept(Accounting, Accounting[country])
   The following is the code in the **Formula Bar**:

   ```
   ✕  ✓  │1  Table3 = AllExcept(Accounting, Accounting[country])
   ```

2. Select and review ⊞ Table 3 located in the field list under the ⊞ Accounting table.

Practice Exercise 111 - New Table Examples

1. This will create a new table from an existing table by specifying certain columns.
   Table4 = Summarize(Accounting, Accounting[Country], Accounting[Customer Name],
      Accounting[Customer Type])
2. This will create a new table based on a Filter.
   SubTable A = CalculateTable(Accounting, Filter(Accounting,Accounting[Country]="Canada"))
3. This will create a new table using a specific column.
   Table 5 = Summarize(Accounting, Accounting [Customer Name], Accounting [Customer Type],
      Accounting[Country])
4. This will create a new table as well as extract the **month name** and **year** from the **CustomerOn**
   Date field.
   Month Name Table = Summarize(Accounting,Accounting[Customer
      Name],Accounting[CustomerOn].[Date],Accounting[CustomerOn].[Month],
      Accounting[CustomerOn].[Year])
5. This will create a new table based on a condition.
   Condition Table = CalculateTable(Accounting,Accounting[Customer Type]="Large")
6. Here you can create a new table from an existing table and group it by a specific value.
   GroupBY = GroupBy(Accounting,Accounting[Customer Type],"Sales
      Count",Countx(CurrentGroup(),Count(Accounting[GrossSales])))
7. This will create a new table, or construct a new table, from code.
   Table Connector = {
   (,   "Test1",3,Now()),
   (2,   "Test2",7,Today()),
   (Blank(),"Test3",5,Date(2000,12,31))}

Section 5 - Quick Measure

You can use ⊞ **Quick Measure** to quickly and easily create common powerful calculations. **Quick Measure** opens a dialog box, you choose the options, then it creates a new formula to be used in your report. You can see the final **DAX** formula in order to learn the code. The following are the categories of predefined **Quick Measures** that can be generated.

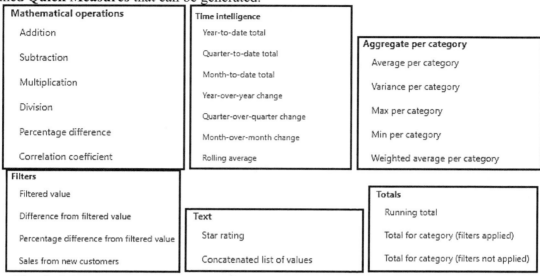

Mathematical operations	Time intelligence	Aggregate per category
Addition	Year-to-date total	Average per category
Subtraction	Quarter-to-date total	Variance per category
Multiplication	Month-to-date total	Max per category
Division	Year-over-year change	Min per category
Percentage difference	Quarter-over-quarter change	Weighted average per category
Correlation coefficient	Month-over-month change	
	Rolling average	

Filters	Text	Totals
Filtered value		Running total
Difference from filtered value	Star rating	Total for category (filters applied)
Percentage difference from filtered value	Concatenated list of values	Total for category (filters not applied)
Sales from new customers		

Tip: The **Quick Measure** features can be created and updated on a regular basis.

Section Table Of Contents

Practice Exercise 112 - Open AccountingA

1. In **Power BI Desktop**: *File Tab →Open →C:\Data\PowerBI-2\AccountingA.pbix →* Open Button.

This will open a **Power BI** file containing the following **Visual Reports**:

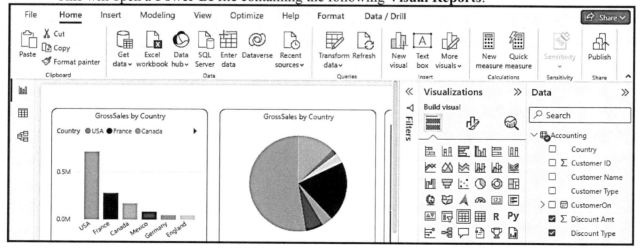

3.19 Quick Measure Methods

There are several ways to create **Quick Measures:**

Method 1 - *Home Ribbon Tab→* 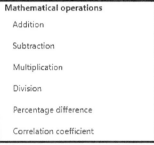 *Quick Measure.*

Method 2 - *Create Table Report→Add Field to table→Press the dropdown arrow in the Bucket→* *Quick Measure.*

Method 3 - *Click the down arrow next to any field→* *Quick Measure.*

3.20 Mathematical Operations

These Quick Measures will create simple **Mathematical Operations** such as **(+, -, *, and /)** to manipulate the values entered.

Subtraction - This uses a **Plus (+)** operator to add 2 separate **Sum** functions together.

Multiplication - This uses a **Multiply (*)** operator to multiply 2 separate **Sum** functions together.

Division - This uses a function to **Divide** two separate **Sum** functions together.

```
Mathematical operations

   Addition

   Subtraction

   Multiplication

   Division

   Percentage difference

   Correlation coefficient
```

Percentage Difference - This uses a function to determine the **Percentage Different** between two separate Sum functions. There are two options to handle blanks:

```
Produce blanks in the output

Treat as zero in the calculation
```

Correlation Coefficient - This uses a function to determine the **Correlation Coefficient.**

Practice Exercise 113 - Quick Measure Mathematical Operations

This uses the **Divide** function to manipulate the **SUM** of the two values entered.

1. *Home Ribbon Tab→* *Quick Measure→(Enter the following):*

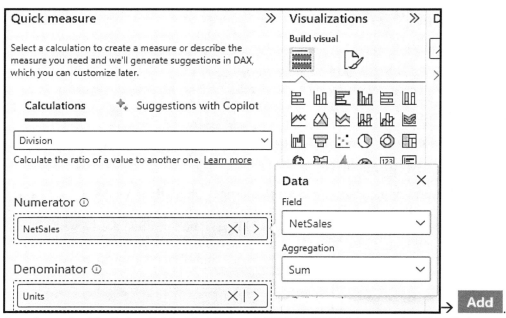

2. Review the code: *NetSales divided by Units =DIVIDE(SUM('Accounting'[NetSales]), SUM('Accounting'[Units]))*
3. Create a Table and add the fields:
    3a. *Click in the white area to unselect all reports.*
    3b.*Select the* ▦ *Table icon.*
    3c. *Add fields:* ☑ Customer Name *and* ☑ ▦ NetSales divided by Units.
4. The final result will look similar to the following:

Customer Name	NetSales divided by Units
7 Bikes For 7 Brothers	18.17
Against The Wind Bikes	34.61
AIC Childrens	2.13
Alley Cat Cycles	4.53
Arsenault et Maurier	9.49
Total	**3.18**

Practice Exercise 114 - Quick Measure Percentage

This will create a **Percentage** value comparing the "**Base Value**" by the "**Value To Compare**" (see the screen to the right).

1. *Home Ribbon Tab* → ▦ *Quick Measures* → (Enter the following):

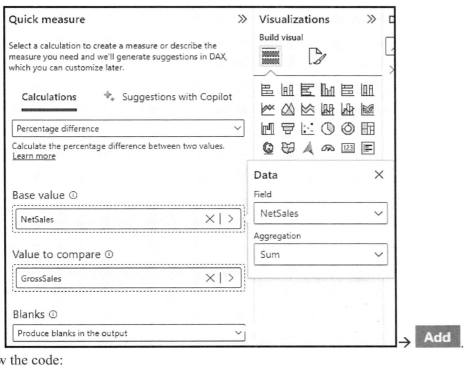

2. Review the code:

```
GrossSales % difference from NetSales =
    VAR  BASELINE_VALUE = SUM('Accounting'[NetSales])
    VAR  VALUE_TO_COMPARE = SUM('Accounting'[GrossSales])
    RETURN
        IF(NOT ISBLANK
            (VALUE_TO_COMPARE),
        DIVIDE(VALUE_TO_COMPARE -
            BASELINE_VALUE,
            BASELINE_VALUE)
        )
```

3. Create a Table and add the fields:

    3a. ***Click in the white area to unselect all reports.***

    3b. ***Select the*** ⊞ ***Table icon.***

    3c. ***Add fields:*** ☑ Customer Name , ☑ Σ GrossSales , ☑ Σ NetSales
    ☑ ▦ GrossSales % difference from NetSales .

4. Format the percentage: ***Select***  →***Measure Tools***

    Ribbon→Formatting Group→ % .

5. The final result will look similar to the following:

Customer Name	GrossSales	NetSales	GrossSales % difference from NetSales
7 Bikes For 7 Brothers	12,030.89	12,030.89	0.00%
Against The Wind Bikes	8,512.94	7,406.26	14.94%
AIC Childrens	1,332.66	1,212.72	9.89%
Alley Cat Cycles	10,350.06	9,729.06	6.38%
Arsenault et Maurier	13,073.80	12,289.37	6.38%
Aruba Sport	13,158.63	13,158.63	0.00%
Total	1,361,660.99	1,260,642.81	8.01%

3.21 Aggregate Per - Category

Aggregate value **Quick Measures** will consider all the data and produce a total amount.
Average Per Category - This will display an **Average** value for each category entered.
Variance Per Category - This will display a **Variance** value for each category entered.
Max Per Category - This will display a **Maximum** value for each category entered.
Min Per Category - This will display a **Minimum** value for each category entered
Weighted Average Per Category - This will display a **Weighted Average** value for each category entered.

```
Aggregate per category

Average per category

Variance per category

Max per category

Min per category

Weighted average per category
```

Practice Exercise 115 - Quick Measure Aggregate Functions

This example will generate the **Average GrossSales Per Category** when you place the result in a table.

1. *Home Ribbon Tab →* 🖩 *Quick Measure →(Enter the following):*

2. Review the code:
   GrossSales average per GrossSales = AVERAGEX(KEEPFILTERS(VALUES('Accounting'[GrossSales])), CALCULATE(SUM('Accounting'[GrossSales])))
3. Create a **Table** and add the fields:
   3a. *Click in the white area to unselect all reports.*
   3b. *Select the* ▦ *Table icon.*
   3c.*Add fields:* ☑ Customer Name *and* ☑ 🖩 GrossSales average per GrossSales
4. The final result will look similar to the following:

Customer Type	GrossSales average per GrossSales
Small	5,914.78
Large	5,682.16
Medium	5,575.98
Small Business	5,545.61
Midmarket	5,534.36
Total	5,894.64

Tip: Another test would be to create a  **New Measure** such as: *AverageGS = Average([GrossSales])* and place it next to the table above.

Customer Type	GrossSales average per GrossSales	AverageGS
Large	5,682.16	5,682.16
Medium	5,575.98	5,466.65
Midmarket	5,534.36	5,534.36
Small	5,914.78	5,791.56
Small Business	5,545.61	5,545.61
Total	5,894.64	5,603.54

3.22 Filters

A **Filter** option will extract a subset of information from a data source. The following are the **Filter Quick Measures** available:

Filtered Value - This will create a formula and will provide the option to **Filter** a specific record.

Difference From Filtered Value - This will create a **Difference From** formula and allow you to apply a Filter to the **Difference From** result.

Filters
Filtered value
Difference from filtered value
Percentage difference from filtered value
Sales from new customers

Percentage Difference From Filtered Value - This will Create a **Percentage Difference From** formula and allow you to apply a **Filter** to the **Percentage Difference From** the result.

Sales From New Customers - This will determine the **Sales** of a **New Customer** field.

Practice Exercise 116 - Quick Measure Filters

This will generate the **Total GrossSales** for a specific **Filtered Customer Type**.

1. *Home Ribbon Tab → Quick Measure →(Enter the following):*

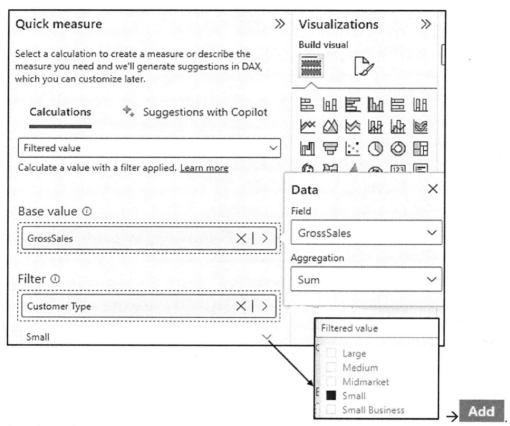

2. Review the code: **GrossSales for Small = CALCULATE(SUM('Accounting'[GrossSales]), 'Accounting'[Customer Type] IN { "Small" })**

3. Create a **Card** and add the fields:

   3a. ***Click in the white area to unselect all reports.***

   3b. ***Select the*** 123 ***Card icon.***

   3c. ***Add field:*** ☑ 🖩 GrossSales For Small

4. The final result will look similar to the following:

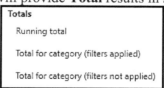

3.23 Totals

The **Totals Quick Measure** category will provide **Total** results in several different ways.

Totals
Running total
Total for category (filters applied)
Total for category (filters not applied)

Running Total - This is a **Sum** in a list that will increase by adding the previous **Sum** to the current **Sum Total.** It will continue to add up for each line in a list.

Total For Category (Filters Applied) - This will display the **Total** value in each category and remove any data that has **Filters** applied.

Total For Category (Filters Not Applied) - This will display the **Total** value in each **Category** and *ignore* the **Filter** that has been applied.

Practice Exercise 117 - Quick Measure Totals

This will generate a **Running Total** for the **Customer Name** field. The total of the first value will be added to the second value.

1. *Home Ribbon Tab →* 📇 *Quick Measures →(Enter the following):*

Quick measure »

Select a calculation to create a measure or describe the measure you need and we'll generate suggestions in DAX, which you can customize later.

Calculations   ✦ Suggestions with Copilot

Running total   ∨

Calculate the running total over a measure in a specific field.
Learn more

Base value ⓘ

| GrossSales   × \| > |

Field ⓘ

| Customer Name   × \| > |

Direction ⓘ

| Ascending   ∨ |

Visualizations »

Build visual

Data   ×

Field

| GrossSales   ∨ |

Aggregation

| Sum   ∨ |

→ **Add** .

2. Review the code:

   GrossSales running total in Customer Name = CALCULATE(SUM('Accounting'[GrossSales]), FILTER(ALLSELECTED('Accounting'[Customer Name]), ISONORAFTER('Accounting'[Customer Name], MAX('Accounting'[Customer Name]), DESC)))

3. Create a Table and add the fields:

   3a. *Click in the white area to unselect all reports.*

   3b. *Select the* ▦ *Table icon.*

   3c. *Add fields:* ☑ Customer Name , ☑ Σ GrossSales , *and*
   ☑ 📇 GrossSales running total in Customer Name

4. The final result will look similar to the following:

Customer Name	GrossSales	GrossSales running total in Customer Name
7 Bikes For 7 Brothers	12,030.89	12,030.89
Against The Wind Bikes	8,512.94	20,543.83
AIC Childrens	1,332.66	21,876.49
Alley Cat Cycles	10,350.06	32,226.55
Arsenault et Maurier	13,073.80	45,300.35
Total	1,361,660.99	1,361,660.99

3.24 Text

The following are a few **Text Quick Measures** to be covered:

Star Rating - This will generate a series of **Stars** to evaluate and rank your data results.

Concatenated List Of Values - When you provide a list of options such as **Customer Type**, all the unique items in a **Card Report** will be displayed.

Text
Star rating
Concatenated list of values

Practice Exercise 118 - Quick Measure Star Rating

Create a **Star Rating** for each customer based on the **Max Revenue** of **$14,000**.

1. *Home Ribbon Tab* → 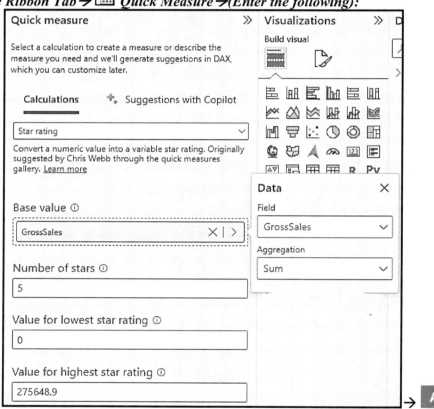 *Quick Measure* → *(Enter the following):*

2. Review the code:

```
GrossSales star rating =
        VAR __MAX_NUMBER_OF_STARS = 5
        VAR __MIN_RATED_VALUE = 0
        VAR __MAX_RATED_VALUE = 275648.90
        VAR __BASE_VALUE = SUM('Accounting'[GrossSales])
        VAR __NORMALIZED_BASE_VALUE =
            MIN(
            MAX(
                DIVIDE(
                    __BASE_VALUE - __MIN_RATED_VALUE,
```

```
                        __MAX_RATED_VALUE - __MIN_RATED_VALUE
            ),
            0
        ),
        1
    )
VAR __STAR_RATING = ROUND(__NORMALIZED_BASE_VALUE * __MAX_NUMBER_OF_STARS, 0)
RETURN
    IF(
        NOT ISBLANK(__BASE_VALUE),
        REPT(UNICHAR(9733), __STAR_RATING)
            & REPT(UNICHAR(9734), __MAX_NUMBER_OF_STARS - __STAR_RATING)
        )
```

3. Create a Table and add the fields:

   3a. ***Click in the white area to unselect all reports.***

   3b. ***Select the*** 🔲 ***Table icon.***

   3c. ***Add fields:*** ☑ Customer Name , ☑ Σ GrossSales , *and* ☑ 🖩 GrossSales Star Rating

4. The final result will look similar to the following:

Customer Name	GrossSales	GrossSales star rating
7 Bikes For 7 Brothers	12,030.89	★★★★☆
Against The Wind Bikes	8,512.94	★★★☆☆
AIC Childrens	1,332.66	☆☆☆☆☆
Alley Cat Cycles	10,350.06	★★★★☆
Arsenault et Maurier	13,073.80	★★★★★
Aruba Sport	13,158.63	★★★★★
Total	1,361,660.99	★★★★★

Practice Exercise 119 - Quick Measure List Of Values

Create a **Card Report** displaying the unique items in a field.

1. ***Home Ribbon Tab*** → 🖩 ***Quick Measure*** → *(Enter the following):*

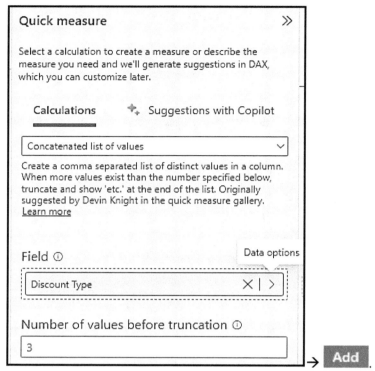

2. Review the code:

```
List of Discount Type values =
VAR DISTINCT_VALUES_COUNT = DISTINCTCOUNT
('Accounting'[Discount Type])
VAR MAX_VALUES_TO_SHOW = 3
RETURN
IF(
DISTINCT_VALUES_COUNT > MAX_VALUES_TO_SHOW,
CONCATENATE(
CONCATENATEX(
        TOPN(
            MAX_VALUES_TO_SHOW,
            VALUES('Accounting'[Discount
Type]),              'Accounting'[Discount Type], ASC    ),
        'Accounting'[Discount Type],", ",
        'Accounting'[Discount Type], ASC    ),", etc."
    ),
    CONCATENATEX(
        VALUES('Accounting'[Discount Type]),
        'Accounting'[Discount Type],
        ", ",
        'Accounting'[Discount Type],
        ASC
    )
)
```

3. Create a **Card** and add the field:

    3a. ***Click in the white area to unselect all reports.***

3b. ***Select the*** 📇 ***Card icon.***
3c. ***Add field:*** ☑ 🏢 List of Discount Type Values .
4. The final result will look similar to the following:

Low, Medium, None
List of Discount Type values

3.25 Time Intelligence

These **Quick Measures** will manipulate **Dates**.

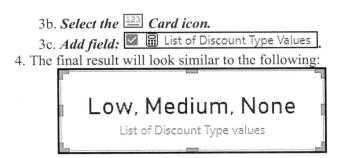

Time intelligence

Year-to-date total

Quarter-to-date total

Month-to-date total

Year-over-year change

Quarter-over-quarter change

Month-over-month change

Rolling average

Year-To-Date Total - This is the period from the beginning of the **Current Year** to the **Current Date**. This formula doesn't work if your fiscal year start date is not January 1.

Quarter-To-Date Total - This is the period from the beginning of the **Current Quarter** to the **Current Date**.

Month-To-Date Total - This is the period from the beginning of the **Current Month** to the **Current Date**.

Year-Over-Year Change - This returns a 12-month period from the beginning 12-months from the current month to the last day of the **Current Month**.

Quarter-Over-Quarter Change - This returns a 3-month period from the beginning of the **Quarter** to the last day of the **Current Quarter**.

Month-Over-Month Change - This returns a 1-month period from the beginning of the **Month** to the last day of the **Current Month**.

Rolling Average - This is an **Average** in a list that will increase by adding the previous **Average** to the **Current Average Total**. It will continue to add up for each line in a list. This is sometimes called **Rolling** or **Running Average**.

Chapter 4 - DAX Reference Guide

In this chapter, we will document many common functions and provide practice exercises to demonstrate **DAX** capabilities.

Chapter Table Of Contents:

Section 1 - Math And Statistical Functions

This section will focus on **Statistical Aggregate Functions** which will process data in columns of a table similar to **Excel** functions such as Sum, Average, Min, Count, etc. **Mathematical** functions in **DAX** are similar to **Excel's Mathematical** and **Trigonometric** functions.

Section Table Of Contents

Practice Exercise 120 - Get Data BikeDB-B

In **Power BI Desktop:**

1. **New Blank Report:** *Start Power BI Desktop or a new blank report (File Tab → New New).*

2. **Get Data and Open:** *Home Ribbon Tab → Get Data dropdown → Excel →*
   C:\Data\PowerBI-2\BikeDB-B.xlsx → Open Button.

3. **Select Sheets:** *Select all 3 Sheets from Excel → Load Button.*

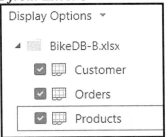

This will **Load** the data directly to the **Power BI Visual Editor** in order to build **DAX** formulas.

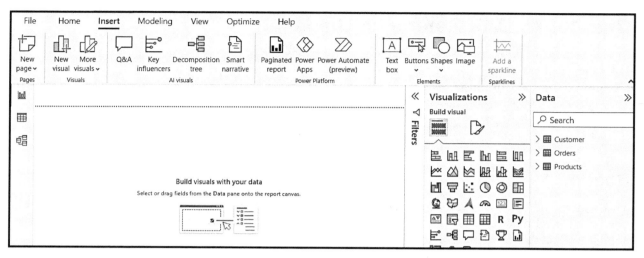

4.1 SUM Function

This is a standard function used to **Sum** up a group of numbers (in a column). When several columns need to be processed, this function will **Sum** each column individually. Then, the column totals can be processed. This is very similar to how the **Excel Sum** function operates.

In the following example, the columns will be added up first, then the answers will be multiplied.

Qty	Unit Price
2	5
4	2
3	6
9	13

Tip: When the **Sum** function adds up the **Column** it will ignore spaces and text located in the database columns.

In this example, the **Qty** will be added **(2+4+3=9)**, the **Unit Price** will be added **(5+2+6=13)**, then you may need to multiply the results **(9*13 = 117).**

The format for the **Sum** function is: *=SUM(<Table[Column]>)*

The following is an example **Measure** stored in the **Customer Table**:

> *Total Sales Sum1 = Sum(Customer[Last Year's Sales])*1.15*

Practice Exercise 121 - Sum Function

Here. we will create a new column and then sum it up. **Tip:** In **Power BI Desktop,** you should already have **BikeDB-B** data source open.

1. **Select Orders Field List:** *Select any field in the Orders Field List (located on the right-side of the interface).*

2. **New Column:** *Modeling Ribbon Tab* ➔ ⊞ *New Column* ➔ *Enter the following:*
   Line Sales Total = Orders[Quantity] * Orders[Unit Price] ➔ ☑ *Commit.*
   The following is the code in the **Formula Bar:**

   ```
   ✗   ✓   Line Sales Total = Orders[Quantity] * Orders[Unit Price]
   ```

   Tip: Make sure you choose ⊞ **New Column** for above and **Measure** for below.
   Tip: To view the ⊞ **New Column** go to the ⊞ **Table View.**

3. **Select Orders Field List:** *Select any field in the Orders Field List (located on the right side of the interface).*

4. **New Measure:** *Modeling Ribbon Tab* → ▦ *New Measure* → *Enter the following:*
   Total Sales Sum = Sum(Orders[Line Sales Total]) → ☑ ***Commit.***
   The following is the code in the **Formula Bar**:

✕ ✓	Total Sales Sum = Sum(Orders[Line Sales Total])

5. **Create two cards:** Fields: Total Sales Sum, and Fields: Line Sales Total.

4.63M	4.63M
Line Sales Total	Total Sales Sum

4.2 SUMX Function

This function will process each row of a table across the columns to perform a math operation. Then, it adds up each final row answer to generate the final result. The following will explain how the numbers are calculated.

Qty	UnitPrice	Total
2	5	10
4	2	8
3	6	18
9	13	36

Tip: When the **SumX** function adds the records, it will ignore spaces and text.

In this example, the expression will process each row by multiplying the **Qty (2)** times **Unit Price (5)** to obtain the **Total (10)**. Once the total for the row is complete, it will then add up the totals of **10+8+18 = 36** (see above).

The format for the **SUMX** Function is: ***SUMX(<Table>, <Expression>).***

The following is an example **Measure** stored in the **Orders Table**:
   Total SumX = SumX(Orders, Orders[Quantity]*Orders[Unit Price])

Practice Exercise 122 - SumX Function

Use the **SumX** function to calculate the sum of the **Quantity** times the **Unit Price.**. The results will be the same as the previous example. **Tip:** In **Power BI Desktop,** you should already have **BikeDB-B** data source open.

1. **Select Orders Field List:** *Select any field in the Orders Field List (located on the right-side of the interface).*

2. **New Measure:** *Modeling Ribbon Tab* → ▦ *New Measure* → *Enter the following:*
   Total Sales Sumx =SumX(Orders, Orders[Quantity]*Orders[Unit Price]) → ☑ ***Commit.***
   The following is the code in the **Formula Bar**:

✕ ✓	Total Sales Sumx = SumX(Orders, Orders[Quantity] * Orders[Unit Price])

3. **Create three cards:** Fields: Line Sales Total, Fields: Total Sales Sum, and Fields: Total Sales SumX.

4.63M	4.63M	4.63M
Line Sales Total	Total Sales Sum	Total Sales Sumx

4. **Create a Clustered Column Chart:** Create a ▥ **Clustered Column Chart** to view the results:

   4a. *Select the white area to start a new report* → ▥ *Clustered Column Bar Chart* → *Add the following fields to the Fields bucket:*

Tip: All the numeric values are the same (see chart below).

5. The **Reports** will look similar to the following:

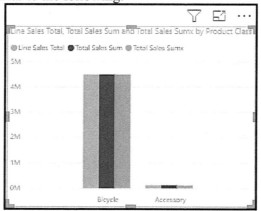

Tip: You need to decide when to use a **New Column** or **New Measure**. If you get an error message, consider using a different type of formula.

Practice Exercise 123 - Sum Problem

As a side note, the **Sum** function will not work in the following situation because of the way it processes the data in a column.

1. The following formulas will not generate the correct answer:

Modeling Ribbon Tab→ 🔲 *New Measure→Enter the following:*

*Total Sales Sum1 = Sum(Orders[Quantity]) * Sum(Orders[Unit Price])* → ☑ *Commit.*
The following is the code in the **Formula Bar**:

```
1  Total Sales Sum1 = Sum(Orders[Quantity]) * Sum(Orders[Unit Price])
```

2. The following will not ☑ check properly: *Modeling Ribbon Tab →* 🔲 *New Measure→Enter the following:*

*Total Sales Sum2 = Sum(Orders[Quantity] * Orders[Unit Price])* → ☑ *Commit.*3.
The following is the code in the **Formula Bar**:

```
1 Total Sales Sum2 = Sum(Orders[Quantity] * Orders[Unit Price])
   The SUM function only accepts a column reference as an argument.
```

Tip: If the **Sum** function does not work, try using the **SumX** function.

4.3 AVERAGE Function

This function **Averages** a column of numbers. It will ignore any space or text that exists in the column.
The format for the *Average* Function is: *Average(<Table[Column]>)*
The following is an example **Measure** stored in the **Customer Table**:
   Average Total1 = Average(Customer[Last Year's Sales])

Practice Exercise 124 - Average Function

Use the **Average** function to determine the **Average** of the **Orders[Total]** field.
Tip: In Power BI Desktop you should have **BikeDB-B** data source open.
1. **Unselect all Reports:** *Select any field in the Orders Field List (located on the right side of the interface).*

2. **New Measure:** *Modeling Ribbon Tab →* 🔢 *New Measure →Enter the following:*
   Average Total2 = Average(Orders[Total]) → ☑ *Commit.*
   The following is the code in the **Formula Bar**:

```
✕  ✓ |  Average Total = Average(Orders[Total])
```

3. **Create a Card**: *Select the white area to start a new report →*🔢 *Card icon →Add the field "Average Total" in the Fields bucket.* The **Card** will look similar to the following:

2.11K
Average Total2

4.4 COUNT Function

This function **Counts** the number of records in a column that are not blank. It is different from the **Excel Count** function which only counts numbers. This function will count a space character or a text label or numeric value, but it will not count a blank cell. The format for the *Count* Function is: *Count(<Table[Column]>)*
The following is an example **Measure** stored in the **Products Table**:
   Count Products = Count(Products[Product ID])

Practice Exercise 125 - Count Function

Use the **Count** function to determine the number of **Customers** in the data source.
Tip: In Power BI Desktop you should have **BikeDB-B** data source open.
1. **Select a Field:** *Select any field in the Customer Field List (located on the right side).*

2. **New Measure:** *Modeling Ribbon Tab →* 🔢 *New Measure →Enter the following:*
   Count Customers = Count(Customer[Customer ID]) → ☑ *Commit.*
   The following is the code in the **Formula Bar**:

```
✕  ✓ |  Count Customers = Count(Customer[Customer ID])
```

3. **Create a Card**: *Select the white area to start a new report →* 🔢 *Card icon →Add the field*
   ☑ 🔢 Count Customers *in the Fields bucket.*
4. The **Card** will look similar to the following:

4.5 COUNTA Function

This function **Counts** the number of cells that are not empty (which includes numbers and text). A blank record will not be included in the count. **Tip:** This characteristic is similar to **Excel**.

The format for the **CountA Function** is: *CountA(<Table[Column]>)*

The following is an example **Measure** to count the **Products[Size]** records:

Product Size CountA = CountA(Products[Size])

Practice Exercise 126 - CountA Function

Use the **CountA** function to determine the number of **Products** that have a color associated with them.

Tip: In **Power BI Desktop** you should have **BikeDB-B** data source open.

1. **Select Field:** *Select any field in the Customer Field List (located on the right side).*

2. **New Measure:** *Modeling Ribbon Tab →* 🔲 *New Measure →Enter the following:*
   Product Color CountA = CountA(Products[Color]) → ☑ *Commit.*
   The following is the code in the **Formula Bar**:

   `X ✓ ¦ Product Color CountA = CountA(Products[Color])`

3. **Create a Card:** *Select the white area to start a new report →* 🔢 *Card icon →Add the field*
   ☑ 🔲 Product Color CountA *in the Fields bucket.*

4. The **Card** will look similar to the following:

   Tip: The **Count** of **Products[Color]** is also **19**, but the total records in the **Products Table** are **21**.

   Tip: Use the **DistinctCount** function to get a unique list of colors.

4.6 COUNTBLANK Function

This function will **Count** the number of **Products** that contain blank records in the column.

The **Excel** formula looks like the following: **=Countblank(A1:A20)**

The format for the *CountBlank Function* is: *CountBlank(<Table[Column]>)*

The following is an example **Measure** to **Count Blank** records in the **Products[Size]** column:

CountBlank Size = CountBlank(Products[Size])

Practice Exercise 127 - CountBlank Function

Use the **Count** function to determine the number of **Blank Colors** in the **Products Table**.

Tip: In **Power BI Desktop** you should have **BikeDB-B** data source open.

1. **Select Field:** *Select any field in the Products Field List (located on the right side).*

2. **New Measure:** *Modeling Ribbon Tab →* 🔲 *New Measure →Enter the following:*
   CountBlank Colors = CountBlank(Products[Color]) → ☑ *Commit.*
   The following is the code in the **Formula Bar**:

   `X ✓ ¦¦ CountBlank Colors = CountBlank(Products[Color])`

3. **Create a Card**: *Select the white area to start a new report → ☷ Card icon →Add the field* ☑ ▦ CountBlank Colors *in the Fields bucket.*
4. *The Card will look similar to the following:*

2
CountBlank Colors

Tip: Another way to get the total of all records:
CountB = CountBlank(Products[Size] + CountA(Products[Size]

4.7 COUNTROWS Function

This function **Counts** the number of **Rows** in the specified table, or a table defined by the table name.
The format for the *CountRows* Function is: *CountRows(<Table>)*
The following is an example **Measure** to **CountRows** in the **Products Table**:
Count Product Rows = CountRows(Products)

Practice Exercise 128 - CountRows Function

Use the **CountRows** function to determine the number of **Rows** in the **Orders Table**.
Tip: In **Power BI Desktop** you should have **BikeDB-B** data source open.
1. **Select Field:** *Select any field in the Orders Field List (located on the right-side interface).*
2. **New Measure:** *Modeling Ribbon Tab→ ☷ New Measure →Enter the following:*
Count Rows = CountRows(Orders) → ☑ Commit.
The following is the code in the **Formula Bar**:

✕ ✓ | Count Rows = CountRows(Orders)

3. **Create a Card**: *Select the white area to start a new report → ☷ Card icon →Add the field* ☑ ▦ Count Rows *in the Fields bucket.*
4. *The Card will look similar to the following:*

2192
Count Rows

4.8 DISTINCTCOUNT Function

The *DistinctCount* function counts the number of distinct/unique values in a column. If there is a duplicate numeric or text value, it will be counted as one. The format for the *DistinctCount* Function is: *DistinctCount(<Table[Column]>)*
The following is a **Measure** to do a **DistinctCount** on the **Products[Color]** column:
Total Product Colors = DistinctCount(Products[Color])

Practice Exercise 129 - DistinctCount Function

Use the **DistinctCount** function to determine the number of unique **Product Names** in the column.
Tip: In **Power BI Desktop** you should have **BikeDB-B** data source open.
1. **Select Field:** *Select any field in the Products Field List (located on the right side).*
2. **New Measure:** *Modeling Ribbon Tab→ ☷ New Measure →Enter the following:*
Total Product Names = DistinctCount(Products[Product Name]) → ☑ Commit.

The following is the code in the **Formula Bar**:

```
Total Product Names = DISTINCTCOUNT(Products[Product Name])
```

3. **Create a Card**: *Select the white area to start a new report* → 🔢 *Card icon* → *Add the field* ☑ 🖩 Total Product Names *in the Fields bucket.*

4. The **Card** will look similar to the following:

```
        7
Total Product Names
```

4.9 DISTINCT Table Function

This function returns a one-column table that contains **Distinct** values from a specified column. In other words, duplicate values are removed, and unique values are stored in the **New Table**. This function could be nested inside another function and passed as a parameter to provide the necessary information.

The format for the **Distinct** Function is: *Distinct(<Column>)*

The following is an example that will create a **New Table** displaying a **Distinct** list of contact position fields: **Customer[Contact Position]**:

Distinct Contact Positions = Distinct(Customer[Contact Position])

Practice Exercise 130 - Distinct Table Function

Use the **Distinct** function to generate a ⊞ **New Table** containing a unique list of **Product Names**.
Tip: In **Power BI Desktop** you should have **BikeDB-B** data source open.

1. **New Table**: *Modeling Ribbon Tab* → ⊞ *New Table* → *Enter the following:*
   Distinct Product Names = Distinct(Products[Product Name]) → ☑ *Commit.*
   The following is the code in the **Formula Bar**:

```
Distinct Product Names = Distinct(Products[Product Name])
```

2. **Table View**: Go to the ⊞ **Table View** to see the ⊞ New Table: ⊞ *Table View* → *Select table* ⊞ Distinct Product Names *located in the field list.*

3. The ⊞ **Table View** will look similar to the following:

4.10 MAX Function

This function finds and displays the **Maximum** value in a column. It ignores blank values and text.
The format for the *Max Function* is: *Max(<Table[Column]>)*
The following is an example to find the **Maximum Orders[Quantity]** ordered:
Max Quantity Ordered = Max(Orders[Quantity])

Practice Exercise 131 - Max Function

Use the **Max** function to determine the **Maximum Unit Price** value.
Tip: In **Power BI Desktop** you should have **BikeDB-B** data source open.

1. **Select Field:** *Select any field in the Orders Field List (located on the right side of the interface).*

2. **New Measure:** *Modeling Ribbon Tab➔* 🖩 *New Measure➔Enter the following:*
   Max Unit Price = Max(Orders[Unit Price]) ➔ ☑ *Commit.*
   The following is the code in the **Formula Bar**:

   ```
   ✗  ✓  |  Max Unit Price = Max(Orders[Unit Price])
   ```

3. **Create a Card:** *Select the white area to start a new report➔* 🔢 *Card icon➔Add the field*
   ☑ 🖩 Max Unit Price *in the Fields bucket.*
   The **Card** will look similar to the following:

   1.85K
   Max Unit Price

4. **To format the 1.85K number:** *Select the* ☑ 🖩 Max Unit Price *in the field list (located on the right side of the interface)* ➔*Modeling Ribbon Tab➔Format Ribbon Group➔Change the Format to $ English (United States),* ⬜ *, and set the decimal places to 0.*

   Data type: Decimal Number ▾
   Format: $ English (United States) ▾
   $ ▾ % ｜ .₀⁸ 0 ↕
   Formatting

   $1,850
   Max Unit Price

4.11 MIN Function

This function returns the smallest numeric value in a column. It ignores blank values and text.
   The format for the *Min Function* is: *Min(<Table[Column]>)*
The following is an example to find the **Minimum Orders[Quantity]** ordered:
   Min Quantity Ordered = Min(Orders[Quantity])

4.12 ROUND Function

This function **Rounds** a number to a specified number of digits.
   The format for the *Round Function* is: *Round(<Number>, <NumDigits>) or*
      Round(<Table[Column]>, <NumDigits>)
The following is a **New Column** example to **Round** the **Orders[Total]** column to one digit: *Round*
   Round Total = Round([Total], 1)   *Before:* 162.87   *After:* 161.7

Practice Exercise 132 - Round Function

The following will round the decimal places to one digit using the **Round** function. If greater than or
   equal to .5 it will round up and if Less than .5 it will round down.
Tip: In **Power BI Desktop** you should have **BikeDB-B** data source open.
1. **Select Field:** *Select any field in the Customer Field List (located on the right side of the interface).*

2. **New Column:** *Modeling Ribbon Tab➔* ▦ *New Column➔Enter the following formula:*
   Round = Round([Last Year's Sales], 1) ➔ ☑ *Commit.*
   The following is the code in the **Formula Bar**:

   ```
   ✗  ✓  |  1  Round = Round([Last Year's Sales], 1)
   ```

3. *See the results above.*

Last Year's Sales ▾	Round ▾
8819.55	8819.6
2409.46	2409.5
298356.22	298356.2
25162.0525	25162.1
33.9	33.9

Student Project A - Math And Statistical Summary

This will summarize every formula used in this sectioin. It will allow you to see the differences and similarizes of the code. Cut and paste the following and create a measure. Then, place them in a table to view the differences.

New Columns:

 Total Sales Sum1 = Sum(Customer[Last Year's Sales])*1.15
 Line Sales Total = Orders[Quantity] * Orders[Unit Price]
 Round Total = Round([Total], 1)
 Round = Round([Last Year's Sales], 1)

New Measures:

 Total Sales Sum = Sum(Orders[Line Sales Total])
 Total Sales Sumx =SumX(Orders, Orders[Quantity]*Orders[Unit Price])
 Average Total1 = Average(Customer[Last Year's Sales])
 Average Total2 = Average(Orders[Total])
 Count Products = Count(Products[Product ID])
 Count Customers = Count(Customer[Customer ID])
 Product Size CountA = CountA(Products[Size])
 Product Color CountA = CountA(Products[Color])
 CountBlank Size = CountBlank(Products[Size])
 CountBlank Colors = CountBlank(Products[Color])
 CountB = CountBlank(Products[Size] + CountA(Products[Size]
 Count Product Rows = CountRows(Products)
 Count Rows = CountRows(Orders)
 Total Product Colors = DistinctCount(Products[Color])
 Total Product Names = DistinctCount(Products[Product Name])
 Max Quantity Ordered = Max(Orders[Quantity])
 Max Unit Price = Max(Orders[Unit Price])
 Min Quantity Ordered = Min(Orders[Quantity])

Tables:

 Distinct Contact Positions = Distinct(Customer[Contact Position])
 Distinct Product Names = Distinct(Products[Product Name])

Section 2 - Formatting Functions

This section will format numeric, date, and time fields to display the proper layout.

Section Table Of Contents

Practice Exercise 133 - Get Data BikeDB-B

In **Power BI Desktop:**

1. **New Blank Report:** *Start Power BI Desktop or a new blank report (File Tab →* New *New).*

2. **Get Data:** *Home Ribbon Tab → Get Data dropdown → Excel →*

   C:\Data\PowerBI-2\BikeDB-B.xlsx → Open *Button.*

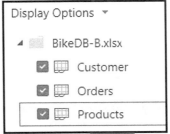

3. **Select Sheets:** *Select all 3 Sheets from Excel →* Load *Button.*
   This will **Load** the data directly to the **Power BI Visual Editor** in order to build formulas.

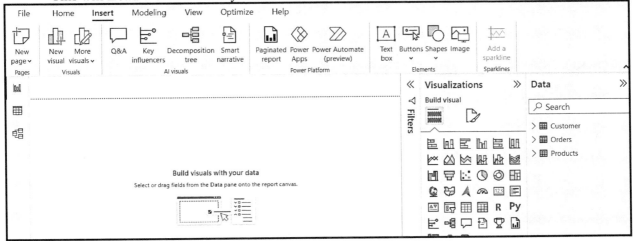

4.13 Format Tools

The **Format Tools** are located in the **Column Tools Ribbon Tab** and are used to format fields in the **Field List** located on the right side of the screen. Once formatted, they can be applied to **Tables** and **Reports**. **Tip**: You must select the field in the **Field List** in order to go to the **Column Tools Ribbon Tab**.

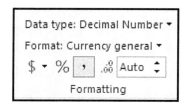

Practice Exercise 134 - Format Tools

Tip: In **Power BI Desktop** you should have **BikeDB-B** data source open.

To format a field: *Select the* 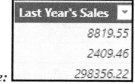 *(located in the field list on the right side of the interface)* →*Column Tools Ribbon Tab* →*Format Ribbon Group* →*Choose the Currency* $\boxed{\$ \cdot}$ *format option* → $\boxed{\text{Currency general}}$.

To review the differences switch to the ⊞ **Table View** and review the $\boxed{\text{Last Year's Sales} \ \cdot}$ column.

Last Year's Sales ▾
8819.55
2409.46
298356.22

Before:

Last Year's Sales ▾
$8,819.55
$2,409.46
$298,356.22

After:

4.14 FORMAT Numbers Function

This will **Format** a numeric value according to the parameter provided.

The following are the available parameters:

General Number - This displays the number with no **thousand** separators. The parameter of **"General Number"** will produce the following results: $\boxed{52809.105}$.

Currency - This places a currency symbol to the far left next to a number. It displays thousandths comma separators with 2-digit decimal places to the right. The parameter of **"Currency"** will produce the following results: $2,345.33 or $\boxed{\$52,809.11}$.

Fixed - This displays at least one number to the left and two digits to the right of a decimal point. The parameter of **"Fixed"** will produce the following results: $\boxed{52809.11}$.

Standard - This displays thousandth comma separators with 2-digit decimal places to the right. The parameter of **"Standard"** will produce the following results: $\boxed{52,809.11}$.

Percent - This displays a number multiplied by 100 and places a 2-digit decimal place to the right. It also places a percent (%) symbol to the far right next to the number. The parameter of **"Percent"** will produce the following results: 25.22% or $\boxed{5280910.50\%}$.

Scientific - This uses a **Scientific** notation providing 2 significant digits. The parameter of **"Scientific"** will produce the following results: $\boxed{5.28E+04}$. The following is an example format: *Format(<Table[Column]>, <Parameter>)*

Practice Exercise 135 - Format Numbers

The following will display several numerical results using the **Format** function.

   Tip: In **Power BI Desktop** you should have **BikeDB-B** data source open.

1. **Select Field:** *Select any field in the Customer Field List (located on the right side of the interface).*

2. **New Column:** *Modeling Ribbon Tab* → ⊞ *New Column* →*Enter the following formulas:*
   General Number = Format([Last Year's Sales], "General Number") → ☑ *Commit.*
   Currency = Format([Last Year's Sales], "Currency") → ☑ *Commit.*

Fixed = Format([Last Year's Sales], "Fixed") → ☑ *Commit.*
Standard = Format([Last Year's Sales], "Standard") → ☑ *Commit.*
Percent = Format([Last Year's Sales], "Percent") → ☑ *Commit.*
Scientific = Format([Last Year's Sales], "Scientific") → ☑ *Commit.*

3. **Table View:** *Display the results in* ▦ *Table View:*

Customer ID	Last Year's Sales	General Number	Currency	Fixed	Standard	Percent	Scientific
132	8819.55	8819.55	$8,819.55	8819.55	8,819.55	881955.00%	8.82E+03
133	2409.46	2409.46	$2,409.46	2409.46	2,409.46	240946.00%	2.41E+03
14	298356.22	298356.22	$298,356.22	298356.22	298,356.22	29835622.00%	2.98E+05
46	25162.0525	25162.0525	$25,162.05	25162.05	25,162.05	2516205.25%	2.52E+04

4.15 FORMAT Boolean Function

This will **Format Boolean** values to display one of the following:
Yes/No - This displays **No** if the number is **0,** otherwise **Yes**. The parameter of *"Yes/No"* will produce the following results: Yes or No.
True/False - This displays **False** if the number is **0,** otherwise it displays **True**. The parameter of *"True/False"* will produce the following results: True or False.
On/Off - This displays **Off** if the number is **0,** otherwise it displays **On**. The parameter of *"On/Off"* will produce the following results: On or Off.
Tip: The following is how you would use the **True/False** field in a formula:
Calculate(Countx(Orders, Orders[Order ID]), Orders[Payment Received]=True)
The format for the **Format** function is: *Format(<Table[Column]>, <Parameter>)*
The following is a **New Column** example to **Format** a column to **True/False**:
Format To TrueFalse = Format([Shipped], "True/False")

Practice Exercise 136 - Format Boolean

The following will display several **Boolean** results using the **Format** function.
1. **Select Field:** *Select any field in the Orders Field List (located on the right side of the interface).*
2. **New Column:** *Modeling Ribbon Tab* → ▦ *New Column* → *Enter the following:*
True To YesNo = Format([Shipped], "Yes/No")
The following is the code in the **Formula Bar**:

```
1 True To YesNo = Format([Shipped], "Yes/No")
```

3. **New Column:** *Modeling Ribbon Tab* → ▦ *New Column* → *Enter the following:*
True To OnOff = Format([Shipped], "On/Off") → ☑ *Commit.*
The following is the code in the **Formula Bar**:

```
1 True To OnOff = Format([Shipped], "On/Off")
```

4. *Display the results in* ▦ *Table View:*

Ship Date	Ship Via	Shipped	True To YesNo	True To OnOff
2/4/2001 3:51:39 PM	Pickup	True	Yes	On
2/6/2001 7:21:39 PM	Loomis	True	Yes	On
12/18/2001	Loomis	True	Yes	On
2/27/2000	Loomis	True	Yes	On

Practice Exercise 137 - Count Payments Received

This uses the **Count** function to determine **Outstanding Invoices**.
Tip: In **Power BI Desktop** you should have **BikeDB-B** data source open.
1. **Select Field:** *Select any field in the Orders Field List (located on the right side of the interface).*

2. **New Measure:** *Modeling Ribbon Tab → ▦ New Measure → Enter the following:*
   Outstanding Payments = Calculate(Countx(Orders, Orders[Order ID]), Orders[Payment Received]=True) → ☑ Commit.
   The formula bar will look similar to the following:

```
Outstanding Payments = Calculate(COUNTX(Orders, Orders[Order ID]), Orders[Payment Received]=true)
```

3. **Create a Card Report:** 〔123〕 *Card icon → Add the* 〔▦ Outstanding Payments〕 *Field to the Card bucket.*
4. *The Card will look similar to the following:*

```
          2069
    Outstanding Payments
```

4.16 FORMAT Custom Numbers Function

This will customize the number of decimals and commas.
Dot Character (.) - The decimal placeholder determines how many digits are displayed to the left and right of the decimal separator. The **Dot Character (.)** used in a parameter of *"0.000"* will produce the following results: 〔52809.105〕. The **Dot Character (.)** used in a parameter of *"0.0"* will produce the following results: 〔8819.6〕.
Comma Character (,) - This character separates thousands from hundreds within a number that has four or more places to the left of the decimal separator. The **Comma Character (,)** used in a parameter of *"000,000.00"* will produce the following results: 〔008,819.55〕. The **Comma Character (,)** used in a parameter of *"###,###.##"* will produce the following results: 〔8,819.55〕.
The following are available parameters:
Zero Character (0.00) - This will display leading zeros before or after the values. If there are more decimal values provided, then it will round them up. The parameter of *"000.000"* will produce the following results: 〔10923.000〕 or〔52809.105〕. The parameter of *"0000000.000"* will produce the following results: 〔0052809.105〕 or 〔0010923.000〕.
Pound Character (#.##) - If the expression has a digit in the position where the # character appears in the format string, it displays the digit; otherwise, it displays nothing in that position. The parameter of *"###.##"* will produce the following results: 〔8819.55〕 *or* 〔4443.8〕. The parameter of *"#.##"* will produce the following results: 〔8819.55〕 or 〔33.9〕.
Percent Character (%) - This multiplies the field by 100. The **Percent Character (%)** is inserted in the position where it appears in the format string. The parameter of *"%"* will produce the following results: 〔5280910.50%〕.

Practice Exercise 138 - Format Custom Numbers

The following will display several results using the **Custom Format** function.
Tip: In **Power BI Desktop** you should have **BikeDB-B** data source open.
1. **Select Field:** *Select any field in the Customer Field List (located on the right side of the interface).*
2. **New Column:** *Modeling Ribbon Tab → ▦ New Column → Enter the following formulas:*

Zero Decimal = Format([Last Year's Sales], 0) → ☑ *Commit.*
Three Decimals = Format([Last Year's Sales], "0.000") → ☑ *Commit.*
Leading Zeros = Format([Last Year's Sales], "000000") → ☑ *Commit.*
One Decimal = Format([Last Year's Sales], "####.#") → ☑ *Commit.*
Format #01 = Format([Last Year's Sales], "#,0.") → ☑ *Commit.*
Format #02 = Format([Last Year's Sales], "#0,.") → ☑ *Commit.*
Format #03 = Format([Last Year's Sales], "#,0,.") → ☑ *Commit.*
Percent2 = Format([Last Year's Sales], "0.00%") → ☑ *Commit.*

3. **Display the results in** ⊞ **Table View:**

Last Year's Sales	Zero Decimal	Three Decimals	Leading Zeros	One Decimal	Format #01	Format #02	Format #03	Percent2
552,809.105	52809	52809.105	052809	52809.1	52,809.	53.	53.	5280910.50%
510,923	10923	10923.000	010923	10923.	10,923.	11.	11.	1092300.00%
518,000	18000	18000.000	018000	18000.	18,000.	18.	18.	1800000.00%
512,000	12000	12000.000	012000	12000.	12,000.	12.	12.	1200000.00%
526,705.65	26706	26705.650	026706	26705.7	26,706.	27.	27.	2670565.00%

4.17 FORMAT Dates Function

This will **Format** a **Date** value according to the parameter provided.

The following are the available parameters:

General Date - This displays the standard date and/or time format. The parameter of **"General Date"** will produce the following results: 12/13/2001 or 2/3/2001 .

Long Date - This displays a date in a long format. The parameter of **"Long Date"** will produce the following results: Saturday, February 3, 2001 .

Short Date - This displays a date using the format d/m/yyyy. The parameter of **"Short Date"** will produce the following results: 12/13/2001 or 2/3/2001 .

Practice Exercise 139 - Format Dates

The following will format several **Dates** using the **Format** function.
Tip: In Power BI Desktop you should have **BikeDB-B** data source open.
1. **Select Field:** *Select any field in the Orders Field List (located on the right side of the interface).*
2. **New Column:** *Modeling Ribbon Tab* → ⊞ *New Column* → *Enter the following formulas:*
   General Date = Format([Order Date], "General Date") → ☑ *Commit.*
   Long Date = Format([Order Date], "Long Date") → ☑ *Commit.*
   Short Date = Format([Order Date], "Short Date") → ☑ *Commit.*
3. **Display the results in** ⊞ **Table View:**

General Date	Long Date	Short Date
2/3/2001	Saturday, February 3, 2001	2/3/2001
2/2/2001	Friday, February 2, 2001	2/2/2001
12/13/2001	Thursday, December 13, 2001	12/13/2001
2/27/2000	Sunday, February 27, 2000	2/27/2000
7/10/2001	Tuesday, July 10, 2001	7/10/2001

4.18 FORMAT Custom Dates Function

This will customize the Date format depending on the parameter provided.
Forward Slash Character (/) - This is the date separator that separates
day, month, and year.
The following are the available parameters:
d/m/yyyy - This displays a single digit for the day and month or 2-digits, if necessary. The year will
be displayed as a 4-digit number. The parameter of *"d/m/yyyy"* will produce the following
results: **5/22/2019 or** 12/13/2001 .
dd/mm/yy - This displays 2-digits for the day and month. A zero will be displayed if the day or
month is a single digit. The year will be displayed as a 2-digit number. The parameter of
"dd/mm/yy" will produce the following results: 03-02-01 .

Practice Exercise 140 - Format Custom Dates

The following will format several dates using the **Format** function.
Tip: In **Power BI Desktop** you should have **BikeDB-B** data source open.
1. **Select Field:** *Select any field in the Orders Field List (located on the right side of the interface).*
2. **New Column:** *Modeling Ribbon Tab →* 🔲 *New Column →Enter the following formulas:*
   Day Of Month = Format([Order Date], "d") → ☑ *Commit.*
   Two Digit Day Format = Format([Order Date], "dd") → ☑ *Commit.*
   Custom Date = Format([Order Date], "dd-mm-yyyy") → ☑ *Commit.*
3. *Display the results in* ▦ *Table View:*

Day Of Month	Two Digit Day Format	Custom Date
3	03	03-02-2001
2	02	02-02-2001
13	13	13-12-2001
27	27	27-02-2000
10	10	10-07-2001

4.19 FORMAT Time Function

This will **Format** a **Time** value according to the parameter provided.
The following are the available parameters:
Long Time - This displays time using hours, minutes, seconds, and **AM/PM** format. The parameter
of *"Long Time"* will produce the following results: 4:00:00 PM , 12:00:00 AM , and
1:00:00 AM .
Medium Time This displays time in a 12-hour format. The parameter of *"Medium Time"* will
produce the following results: 04:00 PM , 12:00 AM , and 01:00 AM .
Short Time - This displays time in a 24-hour format. The parameter of *"Short Time"* will produce
the following results: 16:00 , 00:00 , and 01:00 .

Practice Exercise 141 - Format Time

The following will format the **Time** depending on the parameter provided.

1. **Create a Blank Table:** *Home Ribbon Tab →* 🔲 *Enter Data →(Enter the following Times).*

2. **Table Name**: *Enter Timetable (below) and press Load:*

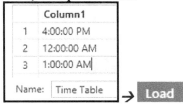

3. **Select Field**: *Select any field in the Timetable Field List (located on the right side of the interface).*

4. **New Column**: *Modeling Ribbon Tab → ⊞ New Column → Enter the following formulas:*
   Long Time = Format([Column1], "Long Time") → ✓ Commit.
   Medium Time = Format([Column1], "Medium Time") → ✓ Commit.
   Short Time = Format([Column1], "Short Time") → ✓ Commit.

5. *Display the results in ⊞ Table View:*

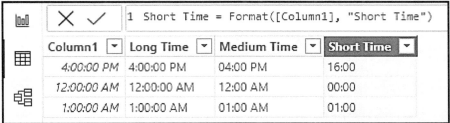

4.20 FORMAT Custom Time Function

The following will customize **Time** depending on the parameter provided.

Colon Character (:) - This is the time **Separator** that separates between hours, minutes, and seconds

The following are the available parameters:

h - This displays the hour as a number without leading zeros using a 12-hour clock.

hh - This displays the **Hour** as a number with leading zeros using a 12-hour clock.

m - This displays the **Minute** as a number without leading zeros.

mm - This displays the **Minute** as a number with leading zeros.

s - This displays the **Second** as a number without leading zeros.

ss - This displays the **Second** as a number with leading zeros.

am/pm - This will use the 12-hour clock to display a lowercase AM for any hour before noon; this will display a lowercase PM with any hour between noon and 11:59 P.M.

a/p - This will use the 12-hour clock to display a lowercase "a" for an hour before noon; this will display a lowercase "p" with an hour between noon and 11:59 P.M. The parameter "a/p" can be either uppercase or lowercase.

AMPM   - This will use the 12-hour clock to display the **AM** string defined by your system with any hour before noon; this will display the **PM** string defined by your system for any hour between noon and 11:59 P.M. **AMPM** can be either uppercase or lowercase, but the case of the string displayed matches the string as defined by your system settings. The default format is **AM/PM**. The parameter "am/pm" can be either uppercase or lowercase.

Practice Exercise 142 - Format Custom Time

The following will format the **Time** depending on the parameter provided.

1. Create a **Blank Table**: *Home Ribbon Tab → ⊞ Enter Data → (Enter the following Times).*

2. **Table Name**: *Enter Custom Time.*
3. **Load**: *Load the new table.*

4. **Select Field**: *Select any field in the Custom Time Field List (located on the right-side of the interface).*
5. **New Column**: *Modeling Ribbon Tab → ⊞ New Column → Enter the following formulas:*
   Custom Time1 = Format([Column1], "ss:mm:ss") → ☑ Commit.
   Custom Time2 = Format([Column1], "HH:MM:SS") → ☑ Commit.
   Custom Time3 = Format([Column1], "mm") → ☑ Commit.
6. *Display the results in ⊞ Table View:*

Column1	Custom Time1	Custom Time2	Custom Time3
4:00:00 PM	00:12:00	16:00:00	12
12:00:00 AM	00:12:00	00:00:00	12
1:00:00 AM	00:12:00	01:00:00	12

`1 Custom Time3 = Format([Column1], "mm")`

4.21 CURRENCY Function

This function evaluates the parameter and returns the result as a **Currency** data type. The format for the **Currency** Function is: *Currency(<Table[Column]>)*

Practice Exercise 143 - Currency Function

The following will format a value to currency using the **Currency** function.
Tip: In **Power BI Desktop** you should have **BikeDB-B** data source open.
1. **Select Field**: *Select any field in the Customer Field List (located on the right side of the interface).*
2. **New Column**: *Modeling Ribbon Tab → ⊞ New Column → Enter the following formula:*
   Currency = Currency([Last Year's Sales]) → ☑ Commit.
3. *Display the results in ⊞ Table View:*

`1 Currency = Currency([Last Year's Sales])`

Customer ID	Customer Name	Last Year's Sales	Currency
132	7 Bikes For 7 Brothers	8819.55	$8,819.55
133	Against The Wind Bikes	2409.46	$2,409.46
14	Alley Cat Cycles	298356.22	$298,356.22
46	Backpedal Cycle Shop	25162.0525	$25,162.0525
117	Barry's Bikes	33.9	$33.9

Student Project B - Formatting Functions Summary

This will summarize every formula used in this sectioin. It will allow you to see the differences and similarizes of the code. Cut and paste the following and create a measure. Then, place them in a table to view the differences.

General Number = Format([Last Year's Sales], "General Number")
Currency = Format([Last Year's Sales], "Currency")
Fixed = Format([Last Year's Sales], "Fixed")
Standard = Format([Last Year's Sales], "Standard")
Percent = Format([Last Year's Sales], "Percent")
Scientific = Format([Last Year's Sales], "Scientific")
New Column: True To YesNo = Format([Shipped], "Yes/No")
New Column: True To OnOff = Format([Shipped], "On/Off")
New Measure: Outstanding Payments = Calculate(COUNTX(Orders, Orders[Order ID]), Orders[Payment Received]=True)
Zero Decimal = Format([Last Year's Sales], 0)
Three Decimals = Format([Last Year's Sales], "0.000")
Leading Zeros = Format([Last Year's Sales], "000000")
One Decimal = Format([Last Year's Sales], "####.#")
Format #01 = Format([Last Year's Sales], "#,0.")
Format #02 = Format([Last Year's Sales], "#0,.")
Format #03 = Format([Last Year's Sales], "#,0,.")
Percent2 = Format([Last Year's Sales], "0.00%")
General Date = Format([Order Date], "General Date")
Long Date = Format([Order Date], "Long Date")
Short Date = Format([Order Date], "Short Date")
Day Of Month = Format([Order Date], "d")
Two Digit Day Format = Format([Order Date], "dd")
Custom Date = Format([Order Date], "dd-mm-yyyy")
Long Time = Format([Ship Date], "Long Time")
Medium Time = Format([Ship Date], "Medium Time")
Short Time = Format([Ship Date], "Short Time")
Custom Time1 = Format([Ship Date], "ss:mm:ss")
Custom Time2 = Format([Ship Date], "HH:MM:SS")
Custom Time3 = Format([Ship Date], "mm")
Currency = Currency([Last Year's Sales])

Section 3 - Specialized DAX Functions

These specialized functions are unique to **DAX Programming** and provide **Filter Context** capabilities. As you process information in a table, you will be able to provide a **Filter** to reduce the amount of data retrieved. You will still be able to provide a summarization of the column, but the **Filter** will provide a subset of the column. Some common **Filter Context** functions include **All, Related, Filter,** and **Calculate.** These can be applied to a ⊞ **New Column,** ▦ **New Measures,** and ⊞ **New Tables** which are different methods used to create formulas in **Power BI.**

Section Table Of Contents

Practice Exercise 144 - Get Data AccountingB

1. ▦ **New Report:** *Start Power BI Desktop or start a new blank report (File Tab →* New *New).*

2. **Get Data:** *Home Ribbon Tab →* 🗗 *Get Data drop-down →* Excel *→ C:\Data\PowerBI-2\AccountingB.xlsx →* Open .

3. **Choose Sheet:** *Choose Accounting Worksheet.*

4. **Load:** Load .

4.22 CALCULATE Function

The primary purpose of the **Calculate** function is to apply a **Filter** to a specific record using an aggregate expression (such as **Sum, Average, Max,** etc.). The format for the **Calculate** function is: *Calculate(<Expression>, <Filter>)*

For example, the **Accounting** data source contains a **Customer Type** field that organizes the **Customer Name** by **Small, Medium,** and **Large** companies. We can use the **Calculate** function to determine the number of **Small** companies in the data source. The first parameter of the **Calculate** function is the aggregate expression such as Sum function. The second parameter is the **Filter** (which *cannot* be a **Measure**). The word **Filter** here refers to the Filter capability of the **Calculate** function. Later we will introduce the **Filter** function which also provides filtering capabilities. The following is the actual formula used to determine two filters, the total number of **Large** companies with an income stream of greater than **10000.**

Example1 = Calculate(Count(Accounting[Customer Name]), Accounting[Customer Type]="Large", Accounting[GrossSales]>10000)

Small Customer Type = CALCULATE(Count(Accounting[Customer Name]), Accounting[Customer Type]="Small")

Practice Exercise 145 - Calculate Function

This will show the **Count** function and compare it to the **Calculate** count capability. This is using the **Calculate** function without a **Filter**. The following two examples will accomplish the same result. In **Power BI Desktop** you should have **AccountingB** data source open.

1. In ▦ **Table View**: 🖩 *Modeling Ribbon Tab➔* 🖩 *New Measure➔ Enter the following code in the formula bar: CountAll = Count(Accounting[Discount Type])* ➔ ☑ *Commit.*
   The following is the code in the **Formula Bar**:

   ```
   1 CountAll = COUNT(Accounting[Discount Type])
   ```

2. In ▦ **Table View**: 🖩 *Modeling Ribbon Tab➔* 🖩 *New Measure➔ Enter the following code in the formula bar:*
   DiscountTypeAll = Calculate(Count(Accounting[Discount Type])) ➔ ☑ *Commit.*
   The following is the code in the **Formula Bar**:

   ```
   1 DiscountTypeAll = CALCULATE(COUNT(Accounting[Discount Type]))
   ```

Tip: In the next example, we will see how to apply **Filters** to the **Calculate** function.

3. **Create a Card**: *Select the white area to start a new report➔* 🔢 *Card icon➔Add the field*
   ☑ 🖩 CountAll *in the Fields bucket.*

4. **Create a Card**: *Select the white area to start a new report➔* 🔢 *Card icon➔Add the field*
   ☑ 🖩 DiscountTypeAll *in the Fields bucket.*

5. The **Card** will look similar to the following and produce the same final value.

243	243
CountAll	DiscountTypeAll

Tip: Sometimes **Quick Measures** add the **Calculate** function when it is not necessary as shown in step 2.

Practice Exercise 146 - Calculate Filter

This will **Count** the **Gross Sales** values within a **Customer Type Report**. In **Power BI Desktop** you should have **AccountingB** data source open.

1. **New Measure:** *Modeling Ribbon Tab➔* 🖩 *New Measure➔ Enter the following code in the formula bar:*
   Customer Calculate = Calculate(Count(Accounting[GrossSales])) ➔ ☑ *Commit.*
   The following is the code in the **Formula Bar**:

   ```
   Customer Calculate = CALCULATE(Count(Accounting[GrossSales]))
   ```

2. **Add Filter:** Add a **Filter** of *[Customer Type]= "Small"* to the **Calculate** function: *Modeling Ribbon Tab➔* 🖩 *New Measure➔ Enter the following code in the formula bar:*
   Customer Small = Calculate(Count(Accounting[GrossSales]), Accounting[Customer Type]="Small") ➔ ☑ *Commit.*
   The following is the code in the **Formula Bar**:

   ```
   Customer Small = CALCULATE(Count(Accounting[GrossSales]),
                    Accounting[Customer Type]="Small")
   ```

3. *Add the* ☑ 🖩 Customer Calculate *and* ☑ 🖩 Customer Small *Measures to a Card:*

243	48
Customer Calculate	Customer Small

4. *As you can see from the results above, the number in the card* ☑ ⊞ Customer Small *is filtered based on the record "Small" Customer Type.*

4.23 FILTER Function

This is usually used to support the **Calculate** function or to filter a ⊞ **New Table**.
The format for the *Filter Function* is: *Filter(<Table>,<Filter>) or Filter(<Table>,<Table[Column]>) or Filter(<Table>,<Table[Column]="Value">)*

It can be used for multiple purposes such as:
1. The result will only be applied to the specific **Filtered** record. An example of a **Filter** used in a **Calculate** function is as follows:
Sum GrossSales of Small = Calculate(Sum(Accounting[GrossSales]), Filter(Accounting, Accounting[Customer Type]="Small"))
2. The second parameter of the **Calculate** function cannot be a **Measure** and the **Filter** function overcomes this limitation (a **Measure** can be used in the **Filter** function). **VarName** below can be a text or numeric field such as "Large" or 450.
VariableExample = Calculate(Count(Accounting[GrossSales]), Filter(Accounting, Accounting[Customer Type]=[VarName]))
3. It can also be used to return a **Table** that represents a subset of another **Table**. An example of a **Filter** used to create a ⊞ **New Table** is as follows:
Table8 = Filter(Accounting, Accounting[Customer Type]="Large")

Practice Exercise 147 - Calculate Variable

In this example, we will use a **Measure** with the value of "**Small**" and we will use this to extract the **Customer Type.** You cannot use a **Measure** for a filter in a **Calculate** function. To work around this, we will use another function called **Filter**. In **Power BI Desktop** you should have **AccountingB** data source open.

1. **New Measure:** *Modeling Ribbon Tab → ⊞ New Measure → Enter the following code in the formula bar: SmallValue = "Small" → ☑ Commit.*

The following is the code in the formula bar:
```
1 SmallValue = "Small"
```

2. **New Measure:** *Modeling Ribbon Tab → ⊞ New Measure → Enter the following code in the formula bar:*
Customer SmallValue = Calculate(Count(Accounting[GrossSales]), Filter(Accounting, Accounting[Customer Type]=[SmallValue])) → ☑ Commit.
The following is the code in the **Formula Bar:**
```
1 Customer Filter1SmallValue = Calculate(Count(Accounting[GrossSales]),
2    Filter(Accounting, Accounting[Customer Type]=[Measure]))
```

3. **Create Two Cards:** *Place SmallValue in Card1 and Customer SmallValue in Card2. The following is the result of all the above Measures:*

4. *The results show if you have a Measure, you must use the Filter function.*

Tip: The following formula will not work because the **Calculate** function does not support using a measure as input to the filter.

> ***Customer SmallValue1 = Calculate(Count(Accounting[GrossSales]), Accounting[Customer Type]=[SmallValue]))***

Practice Exercise 148 - Table Filter Customer Type

This will create a ⊞ **New Table** using the **Filter** function. In **Power BI Desktop** you should have **AccountingB** data source open.

1. **New Table:** *Choose Modeling Ribbon Tab → ⊞ New Table button → Enter the following code in the formula bar:*

   Accounting Small = Filter(Accounting, [Customer Type]="Small") → ☑ Commit.
   The following is the code in the **Formula Bar**:

   ```
   1 Accounting Small = Filter(Accounting, [Customer Type]="Small")
   ```

2. **Table View:** *Display the ⊞ Table View →Click on the Accounting Small Table located in the Field List. The results will display only the Customer Type of "Small."*

Customer ID	Customer Name	Customer Type	Country	Discount Type
236	Ministry of Sports	Small	China	Low
206	Tom's Bikes	Small	England	Low
216	Exeter Cycle Source	Small	England	Low
180	Deportes Perez	Small	Mexico	Low
241	Outdoors Ltda	Small	Mexico	Low

Practice Exercise 149 - Table Filter GrossSales

This will create a ⊞ **New Table** using the **Filter** function. In **Power BI Desktop** you should have **AccountingB** data source open.

1. **New Table:** *Choose Modeling Ribbon Tab → ⊞ New Table button → Enter the following code in the formula bar: Accounting 10000 = Filter(Accounting, [GrossSales]>10000) →☑Commit.*
   The following is the code in the **Formula Bar**:

   ```
   1 Accounting 10000 = Filter(Accounting, [GrossSales]>10000)
   ```

2. **Table View:** *Display the ⊞ Table View →Click on the Accounting Small Table located in the Field List. The results of the new Table View will only display records that contain a GrossSales of 10000 or more.*

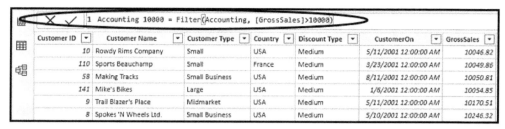

4.24 FILTERS Function

This function called **FILTERS** is similar to the **Filter** function, but it ignores all filters applied to the **Filter Pane**. It will ignore all direct filters applied to the **Filters Pane** in either **Filters On This Visual, Filters On This Page, or Filters On All Pages.**

The format for the **Filters Function** is *Filters(<Column>)*

Example2 = COUNTROWS(FILTERS(Accounting[Customer Name]))

Practice Exercise 150 - Filters Function

This example will ignore all direct filters applied to the **Filters Pane** in **Filters On This Page.**

1. **New Table:** *Choose Modeling Ribbon Tab→* ⊞ *New Table button→ Enter the following code in the formula bar:*
   RemoveAllFilters = COUNTROWS(FILTERS(Accounting[Customer ID])) → ☑ *Commit.*
   The following is the code in the **Formula Bar**:

   ```
   1 RemoveAllFilters = COUNTROWS(FILTERS(Accounting[Customer ID]))
   ```

2. **Create Cards:** *Add the column* ☑ Σ Customer ID *to Card1 and the Measure*
   ☑ ▦ RemoveAllFilters *to Card2:*

243	243
Customer ID	RemoveAllFilters

3. **Apply Filters Pane:**

   Place the ☑ Customer Type to the **Filters On This Page.** Uncheck ☐ Large **Customer Types** (see below).

   Place the ☑ Country in the **Filters On This Page.** Uncheck ☐ **China** and ☐ **England** (see below).

Filters on this page ···	Filters on this page ··
Customer Type is not Large	**Country** ∧ × 🔒 is not China or England
Filter type ⓘ	Filter type ⓘ
Basic filtering ∨	Basic filtering ∨
○ Search	○ Search
■ Select all	■ Select all
☐ Large · 50	☑ Canada · 22
☑ Medium · 51	☐ China · 18
☑ Midmarket · 47	☐ England · 21
	☑ France · 27

4. ***The results will show that the Customer ID card is affected by the filter, but RemoveAllFilters measure ignored the filters in the Filter Pane.***

154	243
Customer ID	RemoveAllFilters

4.25 All Function

This function will extract specific columns in a **Table** and will ignore all **Filters On This Visual**, **Filter On This Page**, and **Filters On All Pages**. If you have **Filters** applied or are not sure what **Filters** will be applied in the future, this function can be used to pull **All** data by ignoring the **Filter**.. The following is an example layout: *All(<Table>[<Column>], [<Column>], [<Column>])*

The following is a **Measure** example using the **All** function:

Example3 = Calculate(Sum(Accounting[NetSales]), All(Accounting[Country]))

Example4 = Calculate(Sum(Accounting[NetSales]), All(Accounting[Country], Accounting[Customer Type], Accounting[Customer Name]))

Practice Exercise 151 - All Function Country

In this example, we will create a **Filter** and apply it to a column. Then we will use the **All** function to ignore filters applied in the **Filters Pane**. In **Power BI Desktop** you should have **AccountingB** data source open.

1. **Create A Table:** *Select the* ⊞ *Table icon and drag the fields* ☑ Country *and* ☑ Σ GrossSales *to the Table.*

Country	GrossSales
Canada	167,284.50
China	26,315.37
England	47,408.82
France	275,648.90
Germany	47,829.84
Mexico	81,136.99
USA	716,036.57
Total	**1,361,660.99**

2. **New Measure:** ⊞ *Table View* → 🖩 *Modeling Ribbon Tab* → 🖩 *New Measure* → *Enter the following code in the formula bar:*

Total GS = Calculate(Sum(Accounting[GrossSales]), All(Accounting[Country])) → ☑ *Commit.*

The following is the code in the **Formula Bar**:

```
Total GS = Calculate(Sum(Accounting[GrossSales]),
                All(Accounting[Country]))
```

3. *Add the TotalGS field to the Table. At this point, the TotalGS and the Subtotal of GrossSales should be the same.*

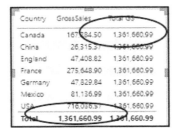

Country	GrossSales	Total GS
Canada	167,284.50	1,361,660.99
China	26,315.37	1,361,660.99
England	47,408.82	1,361,660.99
France	275,648.90	1,361,660.99
Germany	47,829.84	1,361,660.99
Mexico	81,136.99	1,361,660.99
USA	716,036.57	1,361,660.99
Total	1,361,660.99	1,361,660.99

4. **Filter Canada and China:** *Select Table →Filters Pane →Filters On This Visual →* Country *Country Field dropdown →Uncheck ☐ Canada and ☐ China.*

5. ***The result is that the All function disregards the applied Filter and displays the actual total of the*** ☑ Σ GrossSales ***. The subtotal of the GrossSales does not match the TotalGS.***

Country	GrossSales	Total GS
England	47,408.82	1,361,660.99
France	275,648.90	1,361,660.99
Germany	47,829.84	1,361,660.99
Mexico	81,136.99	1,361,660.99
USA	710,056.57	1,361,660.99
Total	1,168,061.12	1,361,660.99

Filters on this visual ...

Country
is not Canada or China

Filter type ⓘ

Basic filtering ⌄

🔍 Search

☑ Select all
☐ Canada   31
☐ China   23
☑ England   26
☑ France   33
☑ Germany   14
☑ Mexico   26
☐ Require single selection

Practice Exercise 152 - All Function Customer Type

In this example, we will extract all **GrossSales** even if a filter was applied in the **Filters Pane** to the **Customer Type** column. In **Power BI Desktop** you should have **AccountingB** data source open.

1. **New Measure:** *Modeling Ribbon Tab → ▦ New Measure → Enter the following code in the formula bar:*
   SumAll = Calculate(Sum(Acccounting. Accounting[GrossSales], All(Accounting[Customer Type])) → ☑ Commit.
   The following is the code in the **Formula Bar**:

```
1 SumAll = CALCULATE(Sum(Accounting[GrossSales]), All(Accounting[Customer Type]))
```

2. **Create two cards:** *Place the GrossSales in Card1 and SumAll formula in Card2.*

1.46M	1.46M
GrossSales	SumAll

3. **Filter Large Customer Type:** *Add the Customer Type column to the Filters On All Pages → Uncheck ☐ Large Customer Type.*

4. *The result is that the SumAll formula will display all records but the GrossSales field will be filtered.*

1.08M	1.46M
GrossSales	SumAll

4.26 ALLEXCEPT Function

This function removes all **Context Filters** applied in the Filter Pane except any **Filters** specified in the in the AllExcept function.. The format for the ***AllExcept* Function** is:
AllExcept(<Table>,<Column>[,<Column>[,...]])

Practice Exercise 153 - AllExcept Function

This will extract all columns in a **Table** except the **Country** column. In **Power BI Desktop** you should have **AccountingB** data source open.

1. **New Measure:** *Choose Modeling Ribbon Tab →* ⊞ *New Table button → Enter the following code in the formula bar:*
   AllExcept = AllExcept(Accounting, Accounting[Country]) *→* ☑ *Commit.*
   The following is the code in the **Formula Bar**:

```
1 AllExcept = ALLEXCEPT(Accounting, Accounting[Country])
```

2. **Table View:** *Display the* ⊞ *Table View →Click on the AllExcept Table located in the Field List.*

3. *The results of the new Table will display all records except the Country column.*

Customer ID	Customer Name	Customer Type	Discount Type	CustomerOn	GrossSales	Discount Amt
132	7 Bikes For 7 Brothers	Medium	Low	9/12/2001 12:00:00 AM	12030.89	0
133	Against The Wind Bikes	Small Business	Low	9/12/2001 12:00:00 AM	8512.94	1106.68
100	Arsenault et Maurier	Small	Low	12/27/2000 12:00:00 AM	13073.8	784.43

4.27 VALUES Function

This function returns a one-column **Table** that containing distinct values from a specified table or column. In other words, duplicate values are removed and unique values are returned. Also, it can be used to pass a generated list to another function. **Tip:** It works similarly to the **Distinct** function.
The format for the ***Values* Function** is: ***Values(<Table>) or Values(<Column>)***

Practice Exercise 154 - Values Function

This will create a **Dynamic Title** based on the **Values** selected in a **Slicer Report**.
In **Power BI Desktop** you should have **AccountingB** data source open.
1. **Create a Clustered Column Chart:** First, let's create a **Clustered Column** and **Slicer** Report:
   1a. *Select the white area to start a new report.*

   1b. *Click on the* **Clustered Column Chart icon.**

   1c. *Drag the fields of Axis:* `Country` *and Value:* `GrossSales` *to the bucket positions.*

   1d. *Click in the white area to start a new report.*

   1e. *Click on the* **Slicer icon.**

   1f. *Drag the Customer Type field:* `Customer Type` *to the Bucket positions.*

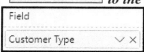

2. *Review the results of the Clustered Column and Slicer Report.*

3. **Create Dynamic Title1:** The following code will create a **Dynamic Title** based on a **Slicer or** select a single value to be displayed in the title. The problem is that it will not display more than one name or the first item in the list.

   3a. *Modeling Ribbon Tab → New Measure → Enter the following DAX:*
   Customer Types Chosen1 = If(IsCrossFiltered(Accounting[Customer Type]),
   "Customer Types: " & FirstNonBlank(Accounting[Customer Type], True)) → ☑ Commit.
   3b. The following is the code in the **Formula Bar:**

```
1  Customer Types Chosen1 = If(IsCrossFiltered(Accounting[Customer Type]),
2     "Customer Types: " & FirstNonBlank(Accounting[Customer Type], True))
```

4. **Create A Card:** Create a **Card Report** and place the **Customer Types Chosen1** field
   4a. *Click in the white area.*

   4b. *Click on the* **Card icon.**
   4c. *Drag the fields to the Fields bucket positions:*

> # Customer Types: Large
> Customer Types Chosen1

   Tip: The ■ Large **Large** should be selected in the **Slicer.**

(Blank)
Customer Types Chosen1

Tip: If nothing is selected in the slicer it will look like:

5. **Create Dynamic Title2:** When you use the **ConcatenateX** function to allow multiple names to be displayed, it tends to repeat the same name multiple times.

    5a. *Modeling Ribbon Tab → ▦ New Measure → Enter the following DAX:*

        Customer Types Chosen2 = If(IsCrossFiltered(Accounting[Customer Type]), "Customer Types: " & ConcatenateX(Accounting, Accounting[Customer Type], ", ")) → ☑ Commit.

    5b. The following is the code in the **Formula Bar:**

```
1 Customer Types Chosen2 = If(IsCrossFiltered(Accounting[Customer Type]),
2 |    "Customer Types: " & ConcatenateX(Accounting, Accounting[Customer Type], ", "))
```

6. **Select Multiple Slicer Fields:** *Hold the* Ctrl *key down and select multiple fields in the Slicer Report:*

Customer Type	Customer Types: Large, Medium, Medium, Medium, Medium, Medium, M...
■ Large	
■ Medium	
☐ Midmarket	
☐ Small	

7. **Create Dynamic Title3:** Now let's use the **Values** command to extract the unique values from the data source to be used in the **Card Report.**

    7a. *Modeling Ribbon Tab → ▦ New Measure → Enter the following DAX:*

        Customer Types Chosen3 = If(IsCrossFiltered(Accounting[Customer Type]), "Customer Types: " & ConcatenateX(Values(Accounting[Customer Type]), Accounting[Customer Type], ", ")) → ☑ Commit.

    7b. The following is the code in the **Formula Bar:**

```
1 Customer Types Chosen3 = If(IsCrossFiltered(Accounting[Customer Type]),
2 |    "Customer Types: " & ConcatenateX(Values(Accounting[Customer Type]),
3 |      Accounting[Customer Type], ", "))
```

8. **Select Multiple Slicer Fields:** *Hold the* Ctrl *key down and select multiple fields:*

Customer Type	**Customer Types: Medium, Large**
■ Large	
■ Medium	Customer Types Chosen3
☐ Midmarket	
☐ Small	

Practice Exercise 155 - Values Table

This will use the **Values** function to generate a ▦ **New Table** containing a unique list. In **Power BI Desktop** you should have **AccountingB** data source open.

1. *Modeling Ribbon Tab → ▦ New Table → Enter the following:*

    Customer Type Values = Values(Accounting[Customer Type]) → ☑ Commit.

    The following is the code in the **Formula Bar:**

```
Customer Type Values = Values(Accounting[Customer Type])
```

2. **Table View:** Go to **Table View** to see the ▦ **New Table:** ▦ *Table View → Select table* ▦ Customer Type Values *located in the field list.*

3. The ⊞ **Table View** will look similar to the following:

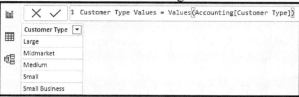

4.28 RELATED Function

This will determine the relationships of several **Tables** and return a column value. It assumes there is a many-to-one relationship between the primary table (where the formula is stored) and the related table (where you can look up a value).

The format for the **Relate** function is: *Relate(<Table[Column]>)*

The following is a practical example of using the **Related** function:

```
Profit Margin = (Orders[Total] - Related(Products[Mfg Price])) * Orders[Quantity]
```

Practice Exercise 156 - Related Function

Tip: We will be using the BikeDB-B data source.

Determine the profit margin by using the total cost of the order and subtracting it from the manufacturing cost. The problem is that the field **Products[Mfg Cost]** is located in a different table.

Tip: In **Power BI Desktop** you should have **BikeDB-B** data source open.

1. **New Measure:** We will start with the obvious approach. Which is comparing the **Orders[Unit Price]** to the **Products[Mfg Price]**. The difference between them is the profit margin. As you will see, the following example *won't* work because the **Products[Mfg Price]** are not in the same **Table**.

   1a. **Select Field:** *Select any field in the Orders Field List (located on the right side of the interface).*

   1b. *Modeling Ribbon Tab→* ⊞ *New Column→ Enter the following DAX:*
   *Profit Margin1 = Orders[Unit Price] * Orders[Quantity] - Products[Mfg Price]* *Orders[Quantity]* → ☑ *Commit.*

   1c. The following is the code in the **Formula Bar**:

   Tip: you will receive the following error:

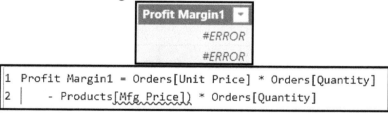

2. **Related Function:** In order to pull a column from a different **Table**, we will use the **Related** function. There is one product but many orders.

   2a. **Select Field:** *Select any field in the Orders Field List (located on the right side of the interface).*

   2b. *Modeling Ribbon Tab→* ⊞ *New Column→ Enter the following DAX:*
   *Profit Margin2 = Orders[Unit Price] * Orders[Quantity] - Related(Products[Mfg Price]) * Orders[Quantity]* → ☑ *Commit.*

   2c. The following is the code in the **Formula Bar**:

```
1 Profit Margin2 = Orders[Unit Price] * Orders[Quantity]
2         - Related(Products[Mfg Price]) * Orders[Quantity]
```

3. *Order Table Results:*

Order ID	Product ID	Unit Price	Quantity	Total	Profit Margin1	Profit Margin2
1254	201161	1592	3	4776	#ERROR	2483.52
1250	201161	1592	3	4776	#ERROR	2483.52
2488	201161	1592	3	4776	#ERROR	2483.52
1371	201161	1592	3	4776	#ERROR	2483.52
1848	201161	1592	3	4776	#ERROR	2483.52
2752	201161	1592	3	4776	#ERROR	2483.52

4.29 RELATEDTABLE

This will allow you to pull data from a different table where there is a **One-To-Many Relationship**. It is the opposite of a **Related** function. In other words, if you have a **Customer Table** and you want to know the number of orders for each customer, you can identify the customer's name and use the **RelatedTable** function to determine how many orders are **Related** to the **Customer**.
The following is a practical example of using the **RelatedTable** function:
Products Sold = CountX(RelatedTable(Orders), (Products[Product ID]))

Practice Exercise 157 - RelatedTable Function

In this example, we want to know the **Count** of all products from a **Related Table**. The **Products Table** contains a list of products, but we need to know how many were sold in order to determine the highest number of sold items.
Tip: In **Power BI Desktop** you should have **BikeDB-B** data source open.
1. **Count Records:** First, we need to do a **Count** of records on a different table.
    1a. **Select Field:** *Select any field in the Products Field List (located on the right side of the interface).*
    1b. *Modeling Ribbon Tab→* ▦ *New Column→ Enter the following DAX:*
    Products Sold = CountX(RelatedTable(Orders), (Products[Product ID]))→ ☑ *Commit.*
    1c. The following is the code in the **Formula Bar**:
    ```
    Products Sold = CountX(RelatedTable(Orders), (Products[Product ID]))
    ```
2. The following is using the **SubTotal** feature in **Excel** to compare with our results. This will be used to make sure our answer is correct in **Power BI**:

	Order ID	Product ID Count	Product ID
96		1101 Count	94
142		1109 Count	45
203		2201 Count	60
291		2206 Count	87

3. **Column Results:** *The Power BI Column produced the following results:*

```
1 Products Sold = CountX(RelatedTable(Orders), (Products[Product ID]))
```

Product ID	Product Name	Color	Size	Product Class	Product Type ID	Mfg Price	Products Sold
1101	Glove	black	lrg	Accessory	5	6.93	94
1109	Glove	black	med	Accessory	5	7.425	45
2201	Helmet	Blue	lrg	Accessory	6	25.872	60
2206	Helmet	Blue	med	Accessory	6	22.638	87
2213	Helmet	red	lrg	Accessory	6	22.638	41

4.30 SELECTEDVALUE

This will return a single value that has been applied to a **Slicer Filter** or **Drillthrough**. You must specify the column in question because if more than one value has been selected, it will return a blank result. This feature can be used to identify what was selected in order to make decisions and this will apply **Conditional Format** to a **Chart Title**.

Practice Exercise 158 - SelectedValue Function

1. **Create a Stacked Column Chart:** [icon] **→Axis: Country Value: Gross Sales.**
2. **Create a Slicer:** [icon] **→Field: Country.**

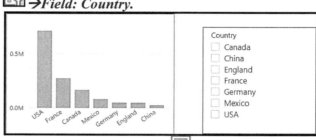

3. **Create a Measure:** *Modeling Ribbon Tab→* [icon] *New Measure→ Enter the following DAX: Line Chart Title = "Countries Selected: " & Selectedvalue(Accounting[Country])* → [✓] *Commit.*

4. The following is the code in the **Formula Bar**:

```
1 Line Chart Title = "Countries Selected: " & Selectedvalue(Accounting[Country])
```

5. **Apply Measure:** *Select the Stacked Column Chart→Format→General→Title→Text:*

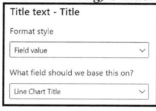

→Fx(Conditional Formatting)→Enter the following:

6. *Select Canada in the Slicer:*

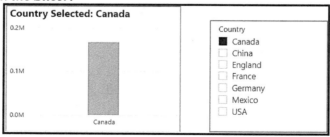

Student Project C - Specialized DAX Functions Summary

This will summarize every formula used in this sectioin. It will allow you to see the differences and similarizes of the code. Cut and paste the following and create a measure. Then, place them in a table to view the differences.

New Columns:

Profit Margin1 = Orders[Unit Price] * Orders[Quantity] - Products[Mfg Price] *
    Orders[Quantity]

Profit Margin2 = Orders[Unit Price] * Orders[Quantity] - Related(Products[Mfg Price]) *
    Orders[Quantity]

Products Sold = CountX(RelatedTable(Orders), (Products[Product ID]))

New Measures
SmallValue = "Small"
Example1 = Calculate(Count(Accounting[Customer Name]), Accounting[Customer
    Type]="Large", Accounting[GrossSales]>10000)
CountAll = Count(Accounting[Discount Type])
DiscountTypeAll = Calculate(Count(Accounting[Discount Type]))
Customer Count = Count(Accounting[GrossSales])
Customer Calculate = Calculate(Count(Accounting[GrossSales]))
Customer Small = Calculate(Count(Accounting[GrossSales]), Accounting[Customer
    Type]="Small")
Sum GrossSales of Small = Calculate(Sum(Accounting[GrossSales]), Filter(Accounting,
    Accounting[Customer Type]="Small"))
VariableExample = Calculate(Count(Accounting[GrossSales]), Filter(Accounting,
    Accounting[Customer Type]=[VarName]))
Customer SmallValue = Calculate(Count(Accounting[GrossSales]), Filter(Accounting,
    Accounting[Customer Type]=[SmallValue]))
Customer SmallValue1 = Calculate(Count(Accounting[GrossSales]), Accounting[Customer
    Type]=[SmallValue]))
Example2 = COUNTROWS(FILTERS(Accounting[Customer Name]))
RemoveAllFilters = COUNTROWS(FILTERS(Accounting[Customer ID]))
Example3 = Calculate(Sum(Accounting[NetSales]), All(Accounting[Country]))
Example4 = Calculate(Sum(Accounting[NetSales]), All(Accounting[Country],
    Accounting[Customer Type], Accounting[Customer Name]))
Total GS = Calculate(Sum(Accounting[GrossSales]), All(Accounting[Country]))
SumAll = Calculate(Sum(Acccounting. Accounting[GrossSales], All(Accounting[Customer
    Type]))
 AllExcept = AllExcept(Accounting, Accounting[Country])
Customer Filter = Calculate(Count(Accounting[GrossSales]), Filter(Accounting,
    Accounting[Customer Type]="Small"))
Large Customer Type = Calculate(Sum(Accounting[GrossSales]), Accounting[Customer Type]
    = "Large")
Unique Values = Calculate(DistinctCount(Accounting[Discount Type]))
Sum GrossSales Of Small = Calculate(Sum(Accounting[GrossSales]), Filter(Accounting,
    Accounting[Customer Type]="Small"))
Total NS = Calculate(Sum(Accounting[NetSales]), All(Accounting[Country]))
Total GS = Calculate(Sum(Accounting[GrossSales]), All(Accounting[Country]))
SumAll = Calculate(Sum(Accounting[GrossSales]), All(Accounting[Customer Type]))
Customer Type Filter = Calculate(Sum(Accounting[GrossSales]), Filter(Accounting,
    All(Accounting[Customer Type])="Medium"))
Product Filter = Calculate(Sum(Accounting[GrossSales]), All(Filter(Accounting,
    Accounting[Customer Type] = "Medium")))
Large Filter = Calculate(Sum(Accounting[GrossSales]), All(Accounting[Customer Type] =
    "Large"))
AllExcept1 = Calculate(Accounting[GrossSales], AllExcept(Accounting, Accounting[Country] =
    "Canada"))

Customer Type Chosen1 = If(ISCrossFiltered(Accounting[CustomerType]), "Customer Types: " & FirstNonBlank(Accounting[Customer Type], True))

Customer Type Chosen2 = If(ISCrossFiltered(Accounting[CustomerType]), "Customer Types: " & ConcatenateX(Values(Accounting[Customer Type]), Accounting[Customer Type], ", "))

Customer Types Chosen3 = If(IsCrossFiltered(Accounting[Customer Type]), "Customer Types: " & ConcatenateX(Values(Accounting[Customer Type]), Accounting[Customer Type], ", "))

New Table: Customer Type Values = Values(Accounting[Customer Type])

Line Chart Title = "Countries Selected: " & Selectedvalue(Accounting[Country])

New Table:

Customer Type Values = Values(Accounting[Customer Type])

New Table: Table8 = Filter(Accounting, Accounting[Customer Type]="Large")

New Table: Accounting Small = Filter(Accounting, Accounting[Customer Type]="Small")

New Table: Accounting 10000 = Filter(Accounting, [GrossSales]>10000)

Appendix A - Keyboard Shortcuts

Keyboard Shortcuts can help navigate **Power BI** reports.

Keyboard Keys Description

Tab - This will move to different **Panels**.

Shift + Tab - This will move to different **Panels** backward.

Ctrl + ? - This will ask a question.

Ctrl + RightArrow - This will interact with a **Slicer**.

LeftArrow - This will collapse a single **Table** in the **Field List**.

RightArrow - This will expand a single **Table** in the **Field List**.

Enter or Space Bar - This will select or de-select an object in the **Field List**.

Esc - This will stop the **Spot Highlight**.

Right-Click - This can be done on any field in the **Field List**.

Alt Shift F10 - This expands the ⋯ **More Options** in the **Field List**.

Arrow Keys - This is used to navigate to different **Visual Reports** and **Fields** in the **Field List**.

Space Bar - This will select a highlighted field to be used in a **Report**.

Alt Left-Arrow - This will **Collapse** a **Field List** when the top-level field is selected.

Alt Shift 1 - This will **Collapse** a **Field List** from any position.

Alt Right-Arrow - This will **Expand** a **Field List** when the top-level field is selected.

Alt Shift 9 - This will **Expands** a **Field List** from any position.

Tip: The **Feb 2021 Update** expanded the **Search Bar** to include commands. Type in the first few characters of a command to test it out.

Index - Power BI Query Editor And DAX Programming

Microsoft Office Courseware

Step-By-Step Training Guides and Workbooks
Available on Amazon.com (Search for author, Jeff Hutchinson)

To review a sample book, see sample video clip, Amazon reviews and to purchase: Go To: https://www.elearnlogic.com. These **Step-By-Step Training Guides** focus on specific learning concepts including brief descriptions as well as many short 2-5 minute exercises for practice. The Table of Contents and Index will allow students to look up desired concepts quickly and easily. These guides are invaluable resources used to build and maintain computer skills for industry, as well as for personal use.

Available in Paperback: $14.95 or Kindle eBook: $9.95

https://www.amazon.com/dp/B09FW4BZDF

https://www.amazon.com/dp/B09F16R2FL

https://www.amazon.com/dp/B09FXGMF44

https://www.amazon.com/dp/B09J8672X1

About the Author

Jeff Hutchinson is a corporate computer trainer and consultant. He teaches **Microsoft** and **Adobe** products from beginning to advanced topics. Jeff has a BS degree from BYU in Computer-Aided Engineering and owned a computer training and consulting firm in San Francisco, California for several years. He currently works as an independent computer instructor and these training guides are based on topics most taught.

Paperback: $14.95, Kindle $9.95

https://www.amazon.com/dp/B0C6BXC9SQ

https://www.amazon.com/dp/B0C6BTM36Z

Available in Paperback: $14.95 or Kindle eBook: $9.95

https://www.amazon.com/dp/B0C6BSW26J

https://www.amazon.com/dp/B0881Z43R7

https://www.amazon.com/dp/B091NC5MB5

https://www.amazon.com/dp/1691229652

Contact Information: Jeff Hutchinson, jeffhutch@elearnlogic.com or (801) 376-6687.
Evaluation copy: http://www.elearnlogic.com/

www.ingramcontent.com/pod-product-compliance
Lightning Source LLC
LaVergne TN
LVHW081756050326
832903LV00027B/1973